The New Strawbale Home

Catherine Wanek

GIBBS SMITH
TO ENRICH AND INSPIRE HUMANKIND
Salt Lake City | Charleston | Santa Fe | Santa Barbara

Neither the publisher nor the author assumes liability for personal injury, property damage, or loss from actions inspired by information in this book. Any construction process can be dangerous, and safety requires skills, using the appropriate materials and taking proper protective measures. Every owner and builder should study reliable literature on strawbale building and should consult with people experienced in this method.

13 12 11 10 09   5 4 3 2 1
First printed in hardbound edition 2003 by Gibbs Smith, Publisher
Text and photographs © 2003 Catherine Wanek

Published by
Gibbs Smith
P.O. Box 667
Layton, Utah 84041

www.gibbs-smith.com
orders: 1.800.835.4993

Designed by Kurt Wahlner
Produced by Modern Grafik

Printed and bound in China
Gibbs Smith books are printed on either recycled, 100% post-
consumer waste, FSC-certified papers or on paper produced
from a 100% certified sustainable forest/controlled wood source.

Library of Congress Cataloging-in-Publication Data

Wanek, Catherine
The new strawbale home / Catherine Wanek. —1st ed.
    p. cm.
ISBN 10: 1-58685-203-5 (hb); 1-4236-0657-4 (pb)
ISBN 13: 978-1-4236-0657-4 (pb)
1. Straw bale houses. I. Title.
TH4818.S77W36 2003
693'.997—dc21
                    2003000822

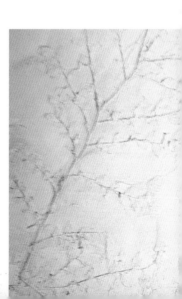

Contents

Acknowledgments

MY GRATITUDE GOES OUT to the people whose homes are displayed in these pages (and many others unrepresented), who opened their lives and living rooms to me and my camera—often sharing a meal or spare bedroom as well. Many of the architects and builders represented in this book also went out of their way to guide me to unique strawbale homes and homeowners that I would never have discovered without their help. Others who deserve a special thank-you for their assistance with this book are Robert Gay, Ben Polley and Laura Taylor, Keith Robertson, Maurice and Joy Bennett, Buddy Williams and Mark Piepkorn. With few exceptions, people choosing to build with bales are eager to share their handiwork and their stories, especially if they think it can help someone else.

In over a decade of involvement with the strawbale building revival, I've been privileged to meet and learn from some of the "gurus" of strawbale, including Judy Knox and Matts Myhrman, Athena and Bill Steen, David Bainbridge, David Eisenberg, Bruce King, Steve Kemble, Carol Escott and many others. On-site and after hours, building discussions have evolved into dear, enduring friendships, spanning time and distance.

Closer to home, I wish to thank my friends and colleagues Marsha Scarbrough and Derek Roff for their editorial assistance, layout artist Satomi Lander for a myriad of computer help, and my husband, Pete Fust, for his advice, moral support and for doing most of the driving.

I deeply appreciate my editor, Madge Baird, for her expert guidance and collaboration, Kurt Wahlner and Lori Whitlock for the elegant graphic design and layout, Johanna Buchert Smith for her attention to detail, and Christopher Robbins and Gibbs Smith for their patience and faith in the material.

This book is dedicated to my mother and father, Betty and Ralph Wanek, whose curiosity and wanderlust have inspired my own, and whose confidence and support encourage me to follow my highest aspirations.

Introduction

A WONDERFUL IRONY about strawbale home owners is that they often started out as complete skeptics. "Doesn't it rot? Doesn't it burn? What about the Big Bad Wolf?" We converts who've heard this before have learned to smile patiently. After all, it was little more than a decade ago that modern-day pioneers seeking affordable, ecological, beautiful housing built the first code-approved strawbale homes. Now they are found in every state in the United States and all over the world.

It's not surprising that so many have been won over by the amazing potential of the humble bale. Individually, stalks of straw seem fragile, but hundreds together, compressed and baled, make a sturdy building block. Stack a bunch of these blocks together and walls can go up in a hurry. Roof and plaster it, and you have an energy-efficient house—the concept is simple and attractive. Plus, soft, sculptable straw bales can be shaped into cozy spaces, forming a home that feels like an embrace.

This home not only feels good, but you can feel good about it; straw is commonly underutilized—composted or burned as an agricultural waste product. The "staff" of the staff of life, straw is available at a cheap price wherever grain is grown. Replacing conventional "stick frame" walls with bales can cut by half the amount of timber needed in a modern home, reducing demand on forest resources. And stacked like giant bricks to form a thick wall, bales offer super insulation from the heat, cold and outside noise, providing a quiet, comfortable living space with modest lifetime energy requirements.

Building with bales could also impact global warming by significantly reducing fossil fuel consumption. And saving fuel saves money. Strawbale home owners from New Mexico to Nova Scotia, California to China, live comfortably with energy bills that are a fraction of their neighbors'.

Constructed with care, these homes have successfully endured snow and rain, earthquakes and hurricanes.

Historical Precedents

Building with bales began over a century ago as pioneers began to settle in the sand hills of Nebraska. Finding themselves in a sea of grass on a treeless prairie, they utilized the relatively new technology of horse-powered baling machines to create a stable building block from an abundant local resource. By simply stacking up interlocking bales and plastering them with mud or cement stucco to create sturdy homes, the pioneers saved their precious trees for roof structures. But as soon as railroads came through, bringing brick and timber and other supplies, Nebraskans began building "real" homes, and strawbale houses faded into history.

Enough examples of strawbale construction survive, however, to give modern builders evidence of durability and confidence in the structural stability of bales.

The Strawbale Revival

While the occasional strawbale building went up in the intervening decades, it was in the 1970s and 1980s that homesteaders, permaculturists and alternative builders, motivated by the potential for affordable and sustainable shelter, began rediscovering the concept of building with bales. The movement may have begun in 1989 in Oracle, Arizona, when Matts Myhrman, Judy Knox, Bill Steen, David Bainbridge and Pliny Fisk got together at James Kalin's house to stack some bales, try some plaster mixes, and test the stability of load-bearing bale walls.

This led to more research and experimentation and a journal called *The Last Straw*, which began gathering information from old and new strawbale pioneers, publishing techniques and success stories, and fostering communication

Built in 1905, the Sturtz ranch house near Stapleton, Nebraska, is one of the oldest surviving strawbale homes. This load-bearing structure is still in excellent condition.

In Huntsville, Alabama, a visionary doctor constructed a mansion of straw bales in 1938, utilizing bales as insulation for walls and ceilings between a concrete post-and-beam structure. As the story goes, Dr. Burritt was making his rounds one day and stopped to rest in a barn. Noting the cool comfort that straw bales provided, he resolved to build this way one day. The result is his legacy, a handsome home with shingled exterior walls, and no hint of its bale insulation. The building has survived over six decades of Deep South humidity and rainfall, and today the mansion serves Huntsville as its city museum.

and cooperation. Within a few years, advocates in both Arizona and New Mexico were lobbying their building-code departments for permits to build bale buildings. They also initiated testing programs to prove the durability of the emerging technology.

By 1993, unplastered, load-bearing, three-string bale wall systems had successfully passed compression, transverse load and racking sheer tests in Tucson, Arizona. And in Albuquerque, New Mexico, plastered, load-bearing, two-tie wall systems withstood a simulated 100-plus miles-per-hour wind force and a two-hour ASTM 119 fire test. The surprised lab technicians reasoned that straw resists combustion when compressed into bales and sealed with plaster because the fire is starved of oxygen. These laboratory results qualify a plastered strawbale wall for a commercial fire rating.

The impressive results of these testing programs helped persuade cautious code officials, and in 1994, Tucson and Pima County, Arizona, adopted a "prescriptive standard" for load-bearing bale construction, while in New Mexico, state officials okayed strawbale building guidelines for post-and-beam structures with straw bales as infill. For better or for worse, these two codes now form the basis of most permitted structures in the United States.

The positive effect of having building codes in place is that they legitimize bales as a building material. Their negative effect is to limit building techniques that can be employed. While strawbale engineering and practices have evolved since 1994, codes have generally remained overly restrictive. Fortunately, a section in most codes allows for "alternative building materials and methods" and gives local code officials fairly broad authority to approve designs that meet standards of health and safety. And in many code jurisdictions across America, strawbale homes have already received building permits, which paves the way for more bale houses in the future.

During the last decade, advocates have developed book, video and Internet resources for learning about strawbale construction, and helping to educate building officials.

Straw-building associations in New Mexico, Texas, Colorado, California and the Midwest offer professional advice and hands-on workshops (see Resources). In California, architects, engineers and politicians recently hammered out the most progressive code language yet, and a state-funded testing program administered by the Environmental Building Network will soon answer more structural questions and offer insight into the relative strength of earthen plasters.

A Home for All Climates

In the meantime, architects and builders have successfully adapted strawbale designs to local climates, from the desert Southwest to the rainforests of the Pacific. The few thousand strawbale homes built in North America in the last decade are generally proving to be durable and comfortable. Strawbale's user-friendly construction techniques can also empower tentative owner/builders to get involved with building their own dream homes.

This is also a house that considers seven generations. Unlike most manufactured building materials, straw is very low in "embodied energy"—the energy required to harvest, process and deliver a material to market. Combined with solar orientation, natural plasters, daylighting, and appropriate ventilation, a strawbale home blends energy efficiency and aesthetics with a healthy indoor environment. It seems that this new/old building technology is poised to enter mainstream consciousness.

So, what does a strawbale house look like? The answer is truly—whatever you want. From southwestern Santa Fe style, to north-country alpine approaches, to sleek urban designs, today's architects and owner/builders are thinking beyond the box and shaping bale structures in response to climate and regional traditions and to suit their personal aesthetic preferences. Look within these pages to discover a wide spectrum of design ideas, plus building insights and hindsights from all across North America. The preferred house of the twenty-first century just might be a strawbale home.

Cost Factors

In the early days of strawbale building, reports that it was dirt cheap abounded, and they persist today. These early reports were not intentionally exaggerated; they just neglected to factor in the sweat equity of determined owner/builders and the savings from scrounging materials. Overall, building a house with bale walls is not so different from any new-home construction. It requires a foundation and a roof, windows and doors, a kitchen and bathrooms, mechanical systems, and a lot of hard work. So it stands to reason that the cost of a strawbale home would be more or less equivalent to conventional construction.

When you ask, "How much will it cost?" the answer is, "It depends." "Price per square foot" is a misleading concept, because there are so many variables in building a new home. Size does matter, and if you think small your overall costs will shrink. It's also true that the not-so-big house can cost just as much as a larger one. One reason is that the kitchen and bathrooms—necessities in homes of all sizes—are the most expensive rooms to build.

Other factors that will increase per-square-foot price include building on a hill, where costs for foundation, structure and labor will be higher. If your property is in the country, far from services and materials, delivery and transportation costs will increase. Building in a city or boomtown, you will likely discover more code requirements and higher wages. Choosing custom windows and kitchen and bath fixtures will naturally increase the price of materials, and if you have a fetish for fancy finishing details, labor costs can skyrocket.

It really is difficult to anticipate all the variables in new-home construction, besides factoring in Murphy's Law. Still, if you understand where the money goes, you can make educated choices to minimize your costs. Your best ally in determining a realistic budget can be your architect or builder. He or she can draw upon experience to help you tell whether your design inspiration matches your pocketbook.

Do Your "Home"work

"Make your mistakes on paper," a wise old building official once advised me, meaning think through the process before you break ground. It's important to analyze your site for access, orientation, views, etc., and visualize your needs. Sketch your own floor plan and collect images of how you'd like your home to look. Architects will often make a scale model of a design before beginning construction.

But don't depend exclusively on a professional's advice. Educate yourself through books, videos and hands-on experience. Your independent investigation into strawbale building will give you confidence and help you communicate with architects, contractors and code officials.

When choosing an architect or contractor, be sure to check out their references. Former clients can vouch for dependability and workmanship. If the architect or builder has no previous experience with strawbale, then their

attitude is crucial. See whether they are willing to learn and can admit they don't know everything. Choose carefully. Your relationship has to endure through the stressful process of construction, so realize it will never get any better than it is at the start. Get a clear agreement in writing and make sure you understand it. Then trust your instincts—if things go sour, cut your losses sooner rather than later.

It's wise to sit down for a roundtable discussion with your contractor/subcontractors before even starting the job. Choose subcontractors who are positive about working with "alternative" materials. Talk over the process with them and ask for their input on how to design each system for quality and efficiency as well as economy. They will have a lot of valuable advice, plus you'll find out about attitudes and how subs might work together. Except for special-ordered materials, avoid giving a big down payment. Once paid for, you have little control over when and how a job is completed. It also makes it harder to cut your losses.

Conversely, be a good client. Be on-site as much as possible, but don't micromanage or you will engender resentment. Respect and appreciate the crew as professionals. It can take time to work out even simple details. Practice your people skills and keep your relationships good. Be responsible to your contractor and pay promptly.

Sweat Equity

If you have more time than money, doing it yourself may be your only option. Keeping your design small and simple and building in stages can allow you to pay as you go without acquiring a mortgage. This way, however, a home can take years to complete, and it requires a lot of hard work, dedication and perseverance. It also takes skill and aptitude. The reward is a home you own completely, and the empowerment and satisfaction of completing the challenge.

Another option is to be your own general contractor. Even with prior building experience, this will be time-consuming and challenging. Still, by hiring subcontractors for critical aspects such as the foundation, structure, roof, plumbing and electrical, and doing the straw-bale and some

finishing work yourself, you can save money while increasing your pride and satisfaction.

Those with busy careers may prefer to hire a professional contractor to build their custom home. This is certainly sensible if you can't do the physical labor or if you have more money than time. Regardless of how much you get involved in the hands-on building, keep in mind that you will have a thousand decisions to make along the way, so be prepared with a clear vision and your mate's agreement.

- Know yourself and your limits—it's harder than you think.
- Be realistic about what you can do yourself and when to hire a professional.
- Know that it will generally cost more and take longer than you think.
- Avoid deadlines. (You can't have it good, cheap *and* fast.)
- Stay on top of your budget; even small purchases add up. Decide if there are some things you can buy later.
- To create good memories, be philosophical and don't sweat the small stuff.
- Try to finish the house before you move in!

Keeping Your Costs Down

As your home design deviates from a rectangle, the price of your roof will increase commensurately. The simplest and cheapest roof by far is a shed roof, followed by a gabled roof. While a second floor can double your square footage for similar foundation and roof expense, trade-offs include a heavier structure and the difficulty of working high up on scaffolding. Dormer windows add style and useable space to upstairs rooms but require significant construction time and a skilled carpenter. Plus, dormer rooms are hard to insulate well and thus will cost more to heat.

Do choose long-lasting roofing, as short-lived roofing materials cost more in the long run. Consider longevity, toxicity, fire resistance, and possible pollution of rain runoff in making your choice of roofing materials. Modern metal roofs come in many styles and colors, are fireproof, and safely harvest rainwater. They are guaranteed for thirty-five years and will often last decades longer.

The absolutely lowest-cost space is just outside your door, on a patio sheltered under the roof overhang or shade structure. Creatively utilizing outdoor areas for living can reduce costly interior space needs. Contemporary homes often combine kitchen, dining and living rooms into one "gathering space," which saves money by eliminating some interior walls. Taller ceilings make a space feel bigger and can create room for loft storage or living space.

Buy standard windows of good quality. While finding bargain windows at factory closeout stores can be fun, mismatched windows often detract from a polished look. When considering used windows, shop carefully. They will be much cheaper but are usually single-paned and in need of some repair. This, plus their increased cost of installation, can easily wipe out any savings.

Remember that not every window needs to open and that having small windows on the north and west (in the northern hemisphere) increases energy efficiency. The premium price paid for argon-filled triple-glazing may be better invested in insulating curtains that also offer shade and privacy. Avoid placing windows at floor level; the low-angled view is rarely exceptional and your R-value (a numeric way of rating insulating effectiveness) will be compromised.

Design to cluster plumbing in common walls and vertically between floors. Carefully plan the layout of lights,

switches and receptacles. Depending on climate, the energy efficiency of a strawbale home often means that you can downsize (possibly even eliminate) heating and/or cooling systems. Check local codes and ask neighbors in strawbale homes how theirs are functioning.

Consider creating a master plan and building in stages. You might build a "guest house" first and move into it, while taking your time constructing your dream home. Or build a small core home, with provisions for expansion. The initial cost will be lower and the experience gained will help every step of the way in your future project. Plus, the more you can pay as you go, the less interest you'll be paying on money borrowed. This could amount to your biggest savings of all.

Home As an Investment

Be aware that even though you think you'll be living in your home the rest of your life, plans can change. It makes sense to consider real-estate norms in your area (e.g., three bedrooms, two baths) when designing your masterpiece. Also, be careful not to burden yourself with a too-high mortgage— the added stress can be personally destructive.

The thickness of a bale wall may be considered a liability to those concerned only with maximum square footage in a home. (For this reason, you will note most featured homes in this book list both interior and exterior square footage.) Of course, when compared with typical stud-frame walls, which have a thickness of about eight inches, this difference becomes less significant. Moreover, wall thickness is what gives strawbale homes their beauty, sense of stability, and

Life cycle Cost and Value

David A. Bainbridge

The definition of sustainable building includes improving comfort and health of the built environment while maximizing use of renewable resources, minimizing life-cycle costs and maximizing life-cycle benefits. The costs of maintaining and operating a building over its projected "lifetime," are the life-cycle costs. The benefits include the economic return and also the productivity, health, and well-being of the users who live in or work in the building. Comparing four sample houses, we can see the impacts design and building choices have on life-cycle cost.

Life cycle costs of four homes, Fresno, California

	Conventional	Strawbale	SB Solar	Owner-built SBS
First cost				
Construction cost	$112,000	$112,000	$112,000	$42,000
Cost to utility*	$8,000	$6,000	$4,000	$4,000

*new generating capacity needed at peak

Annual ownership and operation				
Finance cost annual (4%)	$3,500	$3,500	$3,500	$1,344
Heating and cooling BTUs	37,868	24,892	5,893	5,893
Utility costs annual (10¢kwh)	$1,555	$1,021	$241	$241

Annual opportunity cost (at 5%)**				
Finance (80% of cost)	$4,480	$4,480	$4,480	$1,680
Utility	$400	$300	$200	$200
Utility bill	$78	$51	$12	$12

**opportunity cost is the often-neglected cost of what the money could do if it were invested instead of spent.

This isn't the full cost, which also includes the energy costs of building the power plant, mining the coal, shipping the coal, constructing and repairing the air conditioner, and maintaining the power system. Other environmental costs include nitrogen pollution from nitrous oxides, and asthma, pulmonary disease and other health problems in the vicinity and downwind of the power plant, and significant and far-reaching effects on ecosystems over hundreds of square miles.

Lifetime cost comparison (100 years)

	Conventional	Strawbale	SB solar	Owner-built SBS
Dollars	$1,001,300	$935,200	$843,300	$347,700
CO_2 tons	930	600	140	140

The strawbale solar house would be the healthiest and most economical option because the direct solar heating and climatically adapted cooling is basically free. The owner-built solar strawbale would clearly be the best choice for long-term savings—if the owner could build it. If we had more flexible building codes and gave home photovoltaic installations the same subsidies we give utilities, it would probably be cost-effective to build a solar stand-alone strawbale house with super-efficient appliances. This would dramatically reduce the environmental and health impacts from the house.

Energy estimates adapted from *Alternative Construction*. Elizabeth, L. and C. Adams, 2000. Energy modeling by Jennifer Rennick, energy analyst, San Luis Obispo.

their thermal and sound-insulating qualities. For those who build with bales, this is a trade-off they live with contentedly.

While the concept of strawbale homes is new enough that their resale value is hard to establish, savvy buyers should soon discover their financial advantage. The durable bale/stucco wall system requires minimal maintenance in most climates. And while strawbale's environmental qualities may not be a selling point for all buyers, with inevitable increases in electric and heating costs, the energy savings that super-insulating bale homes provide are sure to be a positive factor for resale value in the future.

Design Essentials

To LIVE UP TO THEIR PROMISE, straw-bale building systems must be understood and optimized.

The number-one nemesis of straw is water, the universal solvent. If exposed to very high levels of moisture, bales (and wood) will support fungal growth and begin to decompose. Wet bales have also been linked to insect infestations, although these seem to disappear as the bales dry out. Conversely, if kept perfectly dry, straw can remain inert for centuries—even millennia. Since the vast majority of failures in houses of any type are directly related to moisture intrusion, it's not surprising that appropriate bale-building design is consistent with good design practice for homes in general.

Straw and wood are similar in composition, and both will rot under the right conditions. The danger point in straw bale walls is generally accepted to be around 20 percent moisture content (above 85 percent relative humidity), sustained for a week or two at warm temperatures. These are the necessary conditions to encourage the growth of fungus that will begin to decompose the straw. Occasional high moisture levels are acceptable, if the bales (and wood) can dry out again.

From Old England comes an expression that describes a well-built home: "Give her a good hat, good shoes and a coat that breathes, and she'll last forever." The "hat" is a long-lasting roof, "shoes" refers to a sturdy, damp-proof foundation, and the "coat that breathes" implies a thick plaster that allows water vapor free movement through the wall system. Just as in centuries-old European buildings, following these traditional design guidelines will prevent most problems with moisture in bale structures.

A "toe up" is commonly two parallel, rot-resistant 2 x 4s bolted to the slab, with the space between them filled with pea gravel or pumice and sprinkled with boric acid and diatomaceous earth to discourage pest entry.

Good Shoes

Long-lasting foundations must be strong enough to support the weight of the building, make it impervious to moisture, and typically extend as deep into the ground as the winter frost depth. If your building site is on a slope, care must be taken to insure that rain and ground moisture have a convenient drainage path around the house. Raising straw bales 6 to 10 inches above grade and installing a moisture barrier (or "damp-proof course") between the stem wall and first course of bales is common practice to prevent moisture wicking up from the ground into the straw.

Besides plain old concrete, effective foundations can be created with mortared stone, a grade beam over a rubble trench, pumicecrete, concrete piers with wooden beams and insulated concrete forms (ICFs). It's best to build the foundation wide enough to support the 1 to 2 inches of heavy plaster on both sides of the bale wall. It's also wise to support straw bale walls a couple of inches above the final floor level, with a "toe up" to prevent an indoor plumbing mishap from soaking the bottom course of bales. In most climates it's cost effective to insulate the foundation and slab from the ground around it—in fact, it's often required by energy codes. While some builders in cold climates have experimented with using bales to insulate below a monolithic

slab, this is not recommended. Monitoring has revealed that bales in contact with the earth will, over time, absorb moisture and eventually decompose.

A Good Hat

A roof design that incorporates wide eaves (two to three feet, if possible) is also highly recommended. Not only will it shed rain and snow far from bale walls, but it will also protect earthen plasters from erosion and cement stucco from becoming water saturated. Additionally, wide overhangs, portals and porches offer the cheapest living/storage space possible and are useful in any climate. Flat roofs and parapet walls, common in the Southwest, are not recommended. Unless their detailing and maintenance is impeccable, they will eventually leak, and cause problems no matter what your wall system.

There is a big difference between vertical and horizontal moisture intrusion. Even a driving rain hitting the sides of an unplastered straw bale wall will not penetrate very far, and the wall will quickly dry out. But water seeping into bales from above will soak down into the middle of the bales, where wall thickness makes it more difficult for moisture to escape.

Proper design and detailing at doors and windows is also critical, as water will find its way into cracks between dissimilar materials. Commonly, windows are set close to the outside of an opening, leaving a wide shelf or window seat on the inside, and the minimum surface needing protection from the weather outside. Where windowsills and ledges are exposed, protect them with a moisture barrier such as tar paper. (This is one of the few places appropriate for sheet-type moisture barriers.) Install drip edges at the top and bottom of openings to shed rain and snow away from bale walls.

Gutters and wide overhangs shed rain and snow away from bale walls.

"... In Ulan Baatar, Mongolia (8 inches of rain/year), I detail for moisture much more casually than in California (20 inches of rain/year) or Oregon (40-60 inches of rain/year). As in any type of building, detailing for strawbale needs to be climate specific."
—*Kelly Lerner, Architect*

A Coat That Breathes

The classic, time-proven, straw bale wall assembly consists of bales with a plaster "skin" applied to both faces. A thick coat of plaster serves multiple functions. Protecting the exterior of straw bale walls from wind, rain and abrasion, it also seals bales from birds, rodents and insects that view them as an attractive home. Inside, plaster provides a smooth finish to bale walls while adding thermal mass. Common choices for exterior plasters include cement/lime, lime, and clay, while interior plasters are often lime, clay, or a commercial gypsum or Structolite product. Consider your climate when deciding which type of plaster to use, as an appropriate design and finish will require minimal maintenance.

It's important to plaster both sides of a straw bale wall to seal out oxygen for fire resistance. For example, if an interior wall were "furred out" with studs to attach drywall without plastering it first, the resulting air space would act as a chimney in case of a fire. A well-sealed bale wall is also critical for energy efficiency, as even minor gaps will allow air infiltration through the bale, reducing its effective R-value.

A cement/lime stucco retains much of the strength of cement and the vapor permeability of lime.

Micaceous clay plaster makes a luscious interior finish.

Breathability—more accurately known as "vapor permeability"—of plasters is also a consideration. While structurally stronger, cement stucco is relatively less permeable than lime or earthen plasters. It is known to absorb moisture from rain, as well as the ground, and wick it into adjacent wood or straw. As long as bales or wood can dry out in time through the stucco, there is little cause for concern. But elastomeric coatings—which are often recommended by contractors because they tend to eliminate small cracks in the stucco—can actually trap moisture in the wall and should be avoided. (In climates with driving rain, a siloxane coating on stucco has been tested to repel moisture without affecting permeability.)

Clay plasters are the most permeable, with the added advantage of being hydrophilic, which means "water loving." Clay readily absorbs moisture and holds onto it, actually wicking moisture away from straw or wood. This accounts for the preservative effect clay has on these materials, making them much less vulnerable to moisture issues. Welsh cob houses and German timber-frame/straw-clay walls provide historical examples of this effect; many such buildings are still occupied after centuries of use. Earthen plasters on straw bale walls may also have this kind of long-term beneficial effect.

Conventional builders often believe they should wrap a strawbale house in an air or sheet barrier (like Tyvek), as this is a standard part of stick-frame construction. This is because stud-framed wall systems covered with gypsum board (also known as drywall or Sheetrock) on the inside and oriented strand board on the outside tend to have many minor cracks where they are joined, which allows air infiltration that compromises comfort and energy efficiency. "House wrap" seals these air gaps and, in theory, repels rain while allowing the smaller water vapor molecule to escape. However, testing results from Canada and elsewhere indicate this product may not live up to all manufacturers' claims.

In a strawbale home, house wrap is not only unnecessary—as a well-detailed plaster eliminates air infiltration—but can be a critical mistake. Such a barrier will prevent the plaster skin from "keying in," or bonding to the straw bales, reducing the wall's structural strength. Worse yet, as warm, moist air migrates from living areas to the colder exterior through the straw bale wall, it will tend to condense on the inside of the exterior housewrap. This liquid moisture will now dry out very slowly, and when the temperature warms, it can produce conditions ripe for fungal growth.

Conventional wood frame buildings also typically employ a sheet-type vapor barrier on the interior to prevent this warm, moist air from infiltrating through surface finishes, into the walls and attic. This practice, however, may lead to a false sense of security, according to some studies. The modern life of a family of four can easily generate 18 gallons of moisture vapor per week into the household air through cooking, bathing and washing. An interior sheet barrier can actually serve as a vapor funnel through any rip or penetration, concentrating moisture at this gap. These small air leaks can create big problems by concentrating moisture vapor in only a few places; when it condenses, the resulting moisture can be significant. In cold climates, the problem can be severe, often resulting in the deterioration of the roof or wall materials of conventional homes.

In a strawbale home, the same principles apply. Plaster finishes, whether earth or cement-based, will offer an adequate air barrier to vapor moving into a wall or ceiling from the interior, as long as potential cracks and crevices are sealed to prevent gross air leakage. Gaps in interior finishes around electrical outlets, overhead fixtures, window and door frames, plumbing, etc., should be well detailed to

reduce or eliminate vapor infiltration. The best strategy for managing indoor moisture is to install mechanical ventilation at the source—in bathrooms, the kitchen and laundry room. Unheated attics and roof systems should also be well vented. Evidence suggests that clay plasters, which can absorb and store large quantities of moisture, can beneficially moderate excess humidity in the home.

Ongoing home maintenance begins with observation. If you have concerns about specific areas, it's wise to install moisture meters or to periodically use a moisture probe in critical spots. Peace of mind is worth the effort.

The Healthy Home

Creating a healthy home involves many considerations, including nontoxic building materials, healthful indoor air quality, and avoiding molds, allergens and pests. Most of us can tolerate modest levels of pollutants in our environments, but some sensitive individuals cannot. And perhaps tolerance is not appropriate, when small exposures can build up to a damaging level over time.

Indoor air-quality problems have a huge impact on our economy and the well-being of millions of people. Modern building materials such as plywood, wood-chip boards and fiberglass insulation are held together with formaldehyde and other toxic glues. Formaldehyde is also found in carpet, which off-gasses for weeks after installation. That wet-paint headache comes from "volatile organic compounds" (VOCs) in the paint formula. PVC and vinyl are fairly inert while in your house, unless a fire starts. When they burn, they release poisonous chlorine gas. The list goes on and on. You can make healthier choices by reading up on nontoxic alternatives and then reading the labels on materials before you buy.

Easy things you can do to improve indoor air quality are:

• Avoid carpeting or choose natural fibers.

• Instead of insulating with fiberglass, try cotton batts (made from recycled blue jeans material) or blown cellulose.

• Use "PEX" tubing, which comes in rolls like garden hose, to replace PVC plumbing parts. This polyethylene tubing costs more but installation can be much quicker.

• If you are concerned about electromagnetic frequencies (EMFs), run electric wires through conduit, and locate your desk, bed and kitchen away from power sources.

"Sick building syndrome" is a product not only of modern materials, but also of naturally occurring "biological air contaminants." The vast majority of molds, fungi and bacteria are benign, but a few, such as the black mold Stachybotrys, can make you sick with flulike symptoms. The key to prevention is to understand how these microbes thrive. Mold and mildew prefer dark places and need moisture, warmth and food. Wet cellulose building materials (carpeting, particle board, plaster board, straw, etc.) can provide a good growing medium. So can the lint that collects in dark, moist heating and ventilation ducts.

• Mold hates sunlight and oxygen, which are naturally antiseptic. So consider a design that allows fresh air and sunshine to help sanitize your indoor environment. And be aware in your design where moisture may build up inside—such as the bathroom. Even a simple exhaust fan can be enough to eliminate mold habitat. Don't wait to repair plumbing leaks or moisture problems, as minor drips can cause major hidden headaches. Left unchecked, mold damages what it feeds on, including your wood-frame structure.

• Avoid forced-air heating and cooling systems, which employ duct work that provides habitat for fungal growth. Though some systems offer excellent filtration for tiny particles, without maintenance they can actually blow moldy dust particles directly into your living/breathing space. Radiant floor heat is silent, superior in comfort, can cost less and requires no duct work.

• The plaster you choose can also play a part in creating a healthy environment. Lime is well known to have antiseptic and antifungal properties, so some homeowners choose it as a finish for bathroom and kitchen walls. (Use caution, it is caustic to work with.) Clay plasters are praised for absorbing odors and softening sounds, and evidence suggests clay is also an air purifier. Earthen plasters can often be made from on-site soil and applied safely with bare hands and without protective eyewear. (You can give yourself a facial at the same time.) Clay plasters will also act to moderate humidity inside homes by absorbing moisture from the air and storing it—providing the perfect humidity range for human health, according to baubiologists.

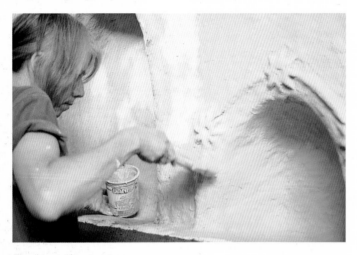

Aliz, or clay slip, is painted on the wall and polished.

Chemical allergies: There's a very low likelihood that chemicals used in growing straw will hang on to have ill effects for individuals who have chemical sensitivities. Straw tested for pesticides showed extremely small amounts of residue; for most grains, chemicals are used early in the growth cycle and then discontinued.

• If you have allergies, a dust mask should protect you during the wall raising, and once the straw bales are sealed with plaster, dust, chemicals and allergens are sealed in, too. Chemically sensitive individuals are happily living in strawbale homes, but for peace of mind spend some time in other strawbale structures before you build your own.

Insects: Compared with wood, few termites make a meal of straw—in fact, there's not one report of termites seen in bale walls. And clean, dry bales typically contain no mold colonies or insects. But like mold, the occasional report of insects can always be traced to wet bales. If insects have laid eggs in bales, moisture will trigger the hatch-out—typically of tiny beetles or mites. These have proven more a nuisance than a serious problem, and fortunately, when the bales dry out, the insects disappear.

• Straw bales should be yellow—avoid using dark, discolored bales, or parts of bales. This means the bale was wet at one time, and the discolored areas will contain dormant fungal spores. Compost those parts in your garden instead of putting them in your wall.

Designing to Your Site

Before you get too far along with a floor plan, spend some time on your building site. Determine directions for solar orientation, and find out which direction stormy weather is likely to come from. Are you subject to winds, waves or seismic activity? Is your site sloped or flat? Where is your access? Where are your views?

It is generally good to preserve existing trees, and you can often utilize existing landscaping to create a beneficial microclimate for your home. Plants can also mitigate drainage problems created by digging your foundation. How do codes, covenants and consideration for neighbors affect your building envelope? The size of your lot and whether it is located in the city or the country will profoundly affect your design decisions, so rather than beginning with a floor plan, start designing from your site.

Interior Space Design

A straw bale wall is like a blank canvas—the finishing touches can be your creation. Rectilinear, round or downright organic, straw bale walls define your space. Builder Turko Semmes, who specializes in thick-walled buildings, says, "Straw bale walls are about the holes, and it's these openings that make it so interesting."

To complement your bale walls, consider natural materials for interior walls. Adobe (hard, sealed earth), cob or straw-clay will create solid partition walls, much thinner than the width of straw bales. All are thermal mass materials that moderate temperatures and work well to stop sound from passing through. Clay, lime and gypsum plasters are textural, sculptable, and healthy finishes. Earth plasters are renowned for their beauty.

An arched doorway with deco
bas-relief opens into a French
provincial bedroom.

A tradition in strawbale building is to have a "truth window"—an opening where the straw can be viewed. The shape and "art" of the truth window is a point of creativity for each homeowner.

If you do it yourself or organize a plastering party, these artistic finishes can be dirt cheap. But if you hire a professional crew, natural plasters will cost more than stucco due to the labor required for the smooth, polished finish. Curvy details can easily exceed the price of straight trim due to the crafting required. Consider spending your money on high-quality materials, while keeping finish details simple.

Utilizing Space

When planning your interiors, pay attention to areas other than the main rooms. For instance, an air-lock entry or mudroom holds some of the most functional square footage in a a house. You can also put to use the vertical space that is often ignored above a flat ceiling and below a pitched roof. Trusses can be designed to allow stand-up room within them, for a sleeping loft or storage.

Flexibility: Consider incorporating an office or bedroom adjacent to the main building, with a separate entrance and bath—perhaps in a daylit basement. Creating a "granny" unit not only provides flexible space for growing children or aging parents but might be rented out for extra income. Many cities are now encouraging attached accessory units as one of the strategies to achieve affordable housing mandates. Check into second-dwelling codes while designing.

Accessibility: Building a universal design—one that is accessible to people with limited mobility—is not only good planning for your future but smart when it comes to resale value. Wheelchair accessibility need not cost much more when it is incorporated from the beginning of the design. Wider 36-inch "zero-step" doorways and lever handles are simple to add in the planning stages. For two-story designs, placing a second-floor closet above a main-floor closet creates a potential space for an elevator addition. Counter and sink heights could be considered as well.

This nicho was custom made for a special piece of art.

Whether formal or casual, a mudroom entry is a useful space that also serves an aesthetic function.

Sound Reasoning

An open floor plan can be visually pleasing, but it can also be noisy. Sound travels very well through air, so door openings, windows and air leaks between rooms become acoustic holes. Standard wood-stud-and-Sheetrock walls also transmit sound via vibration through these materials—between rooms and between floors.

Solid earthen materials work well to dampen sound between rooms. Bale walls also perform well in combination with plaster coatings. Both are excellent acoustic materials that resist both high- and low-frequency sounds. The variety of "straw board" materials manufactured around the country have good acoustical properties as well.

Siting and Energy Efficiency

AN IMPORTANT GOAL of home design is energy efficiency, which means creating a comfortable environment with the minimum input from fossil fuels. Your investment in an energy-miser house is risk free, paying you back in comfort and dollar savings. And as energy prices climb higher, the return is even greater. At least 50 percent of your energy savings can come from simply orienting windows to take advantage of solar energy.

Let the Sunshine In

My favorite architects really understand how sunlight enhances living space. If your site does not allow south/southeast orientation, then skylights, clerestory windows and light tubes are other strategies to illuminate interiors naturally. This saves turning on lights in the daytime, your room will be brighter, and sunshine will enhance your mood.

The benefits of sunlight on human health have long been studied. Natural light has proven to increase productivity and learning potential. Heliotherapy, the controlled exposure of patients to sunlight, is effective against a variety of diseases and was utilized by many doctors and healers, including Florence Nightingale, before antibiotics were discovered. Full spectrum sunlight is essential to our body's manufacture of vitamin D, and "seasonal affective disorder" (SAD) is indicative of the importance of sunlight in maintaining mental health.

The same sunlight also brings in heat. Thanks to the seasonal positions of the sun, south-facing windows can capture heat in the winter and avoid it in the summer. If solar design concepts are included from the beginning, they add little or no extra cost. And the energy savings are significant. However, passive solar requires an active owner—you need to learn when to open your windows and when to close your curtains.

While passive solar design theory demands that homes are oriented within 15 degrees of solar south, buildings oriented at 45 degrees (southeast) can also work well. Having two walls suitable for heat gain gives more interior design flexibility and allows more of a square plan, as opposed to the typical long, narrow, south-facing house.

High clerestory windows on the south allow light and heat into rooms on the north. (Designer: Jeff Ruppert; homeowner: Jim Erdman, Crestone, Colorado.)

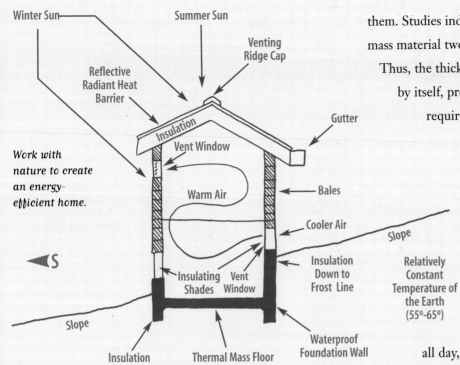

Winter Sun

Summer Sun

Venting Ridge Cap

Reflective Radiant Heat Barrier

Insulation

Gutter

Vent Window

Work with nature to create an energy-efficient home.

Warm Air

Bales

Cooler Air

Slope

Insulating Shades

Vent Window

Insulation Down to Frost Line

Relatively Constant Temperature of the Earth (55°-65°)

S

Slope

Insulation

Thermal Mass Floor Insulated from Below

Waterproof Foundation Wall

Passive solar guidelines will be different as you change climates. In El Paso, Texas, the recommended amount of glass on the south wall is about 7 percent of the home's total square footage, and exceeding this may cause overheating. But in colder climates, designs may require much more glazing. Beware of 1970s solar models—their designs were generally based on conventional 2 x 6 frame walls, so they call for more glass and mass than a super-insulated strawbale structure needs. It's worth studying your site-specific climate, as many cold climates also have cloudy winters, with precious little sunshine. In this context, large south-facing windows will be a net loss. In a tight building with good insulation values, solar heat is only part of the energy-efficiency equation.

Insulate Your Thermal Mass

Once inside your home, the sun's energy is stored in mass floors, walls and objects. Thermal mass materials are typically solid and heavy, and include concrete, brick, stone, earth and water. They equalize to their surrounding air temperatures gradually, tending to moderate the climate around

them. Studies indicate that solar heat can only penetrate a mass material two or three inches during the daily cycle. Thus, the thick interior plaster finish on straw bale walls, by itself, provides a significant part of the thermal mass required for effective solar design. And plaster is distributed throughout the home, creating more even temperatures, without cold spots. Thermal mass can be both a battery for heat in winter and for cool in the summer: if windows are left open to capture the cool night air, then closed in the morning, the coolness stored in the plaster can often keep a home comfortable all day, provided you keep doors and windows shut. A "Trombe wall" can be an effective solar heat–storing strategy, but it works best in the sunbelt. A few cloudy days will give you a large, cold wall.

To optimize the thermal performance of strawbale wall systems, it's important to remember that most heat loss and gain is through the roof. Without ceiling insulation, a strawbale house is like a thermos bottle without a lid. Natural choices for ceiling insulation include blown cellulose made from recycled newspaper and cotton batts made from blue jeans manufacturing scraps. In cold climates, floors and foundations should also be insulated from the ground and outside air. Research in Canada and Montana concluded that it is cost-effective to insulate ceilings to R-60, walls to R-40 and a slab to R-10 in cold climates. About half of the houses in the United States fall into this category.

People rarely find it worth the trouble to use straw bales as roof insulation. Bales are relatively heavy, requiring more strength from your structure and making it a chore to hoist them above your head. Spacing the trusses or rafters so the bales will fit tightly together can require more trusses. It's also essential to plaster all exposed straw as a fire-retarding measure and to discourage rodents from making their home in your attic.

Inside the roof, reduce the gaps caused by the rafters—otherwise the wood becomes a "thermal bridge" for cold or heat. While installing insulation, make sure it fits tightly in the space. Any gaps in the insulation will allow outside air to come through, driven by wind or air pressure.

An Air-tight Envelope

Air infiltration can be a huge component of heat loss. If the gaps around doors, windows, pipes, conduit or vents (or through the wall itself) amounted to 5 percent of your wall surface, your R-value would be reduced by 50 percent! Sealing straw bales on both sides with a thick plaster coat creates a homogenous surface that eliminates infiltration through the wall itself. But anywhere dissimilar materials meet is potential for a crack. Take care to seal these—especially the joints where all dissimilar wall/ceiling/floor materials meet. Tight windows and doors, sealed with weather stripping and caulk, are important components to a super-insulated envelope. Your diligence will pay off.

One drawback to a tight house is that it seals us in with all the smells and moisture from our lives, and away from fresh, oxygenated outdoor air, which is essential to our health. The solution is to build as tight as you can but have a separate ventilation scheme. This can include windows that open, exhaust fans and air-to-air heat exchangers, also known as heat recovery ventilators. Uncontrolled infiltration will also bring in fresh air, but again, it can seriously affect your comfort level and energy bills.

Homeowners should be aware that moisture could build up indoors in a tight house, as water vapor is not escaping through the typical cracks. This warm, moist air will condense on ceilings and especially on cold windows, where it can build up, drip down and stain wooden windowsills. Again, source ventilation in humid areas may be adequate, but in cold climates, a heat recovery ventilation system—which warms fresh, incoming air with the warmth of outgoing air—could be the best solution. The up-front cost of such a system will often pay for itself within a few years, due to the heat energy saved. Also, moisture can easily

collect in unheated attic space, so be sure to vent your roof with soffits and ridge vents.

"What about 'breathable' plasters?" you might ask. Well, these plasters do not really breathe; they actually sweat—that is, they allow water vapor to transpire, or slowly move through the wall system, as nature seeks to equalize indoor/outdoor humidity. That's why permeability of exterior plaster is critical: you don't want the vapor condensing inside your straw bale wall. However, a thick layer of porous earthen or gypsum interior plaster is well known to absorb large quantities of moisture vapor, and can be part of an effective humidity-control strategy.

Windows in Your Wall

Windows are one of your biggest aesthetic decisions, as they define your architectural style, interior shape and view of the world. Your visual connection with the landscape can be enhanced with large windows, or a sense of privacy created with multiple small panes. Windows also perform quite a few functions—some all at the same time. It's helpful to think about the placement of your windows in regard to light, heat, views and ventilation.

Light. Orientation, placement, size and shape of windows will affect the amount of light they allow into a room: the taller the window, the deeper light will penetrate. A south-facing window brings in the most direct light, while windows oriented north provide soft, diffused light. Reflections from interior surfaces also affect light distribution. A white wall reflects as much as 90 percent of the light, while dark colors absorb light (and heat). South-facing clerestory windows bring natural light (and heat) into north rooms in the wintertime, when it is most precious. Skylights deliver the most light for a given glazed area. But in a sunny climate they can be a source of overheating, as well as heat loss, so use them sparingly.

Heat. South-facing windows are preferred to capture winter heat, because a modest overhang will keep the sun out during the summer. But east and west windows allow direct gain, too—it is just harder to control overheating in

A skylight with insulated "Skylid" allows control of light and heat. As a gas heats up and expands, the Skylid opens, and at the end of the day, as the gas cools, the Skylid closes.

the spring, summer and fall as the sun sinks slowly in the west. Seasonal strategies such as awnings or landscaping can mitigate this, while maximizing passive gain in the winter.

Ventilation. Tap in to the prevailing breeze for natural ventilation. For cooling, think cross ventilation, with your intake low on the cool north side and warm air venting high on the downwind side through a window or operable skylight. In many climates, strawbale homes can avoid a separate cooling system, because simple nighttime venting and the super insulation of the bale walls eliminate the need. Code may also require windows that open as an emergency escape hatch. But not every window needs to open. Once you plan your ventilation strategy, you may decide that at least half or more of your windows can be fixed in place, which would produce a great cost savings.

Even the most expensive windows have a poor R-value compared with bale walls. Argon gas and "low-e" films are touted as terrific advances—and they are—but their relative cost-to-value should be evaluated. For instance, insulated window coverings may be more cost-effective than paying a premium for glazing components above standard double-glazing. Also, having fewer large windows will cost less than an equivalent area of small windows, and require less trim work. As a rule of thumb for the northern hemisphere, place the most glazing on the south, ample glass on the east, and the fewest windows to the north and west.

In the Sonoran Desert, a ramada at the Paca de Paja Bed and Breakfast provides an outdoor living space and permanent shade for the west side of the structure.

View. Sometimes your view demands a picture window—so go for it! No matter what direction it faces, you will want the ability to allow in the sun's light and heat, or keep them out. And in most climates, you'll want to be able to insulate from cold, too, so be thinking of your curtain strategy right up front.

Roman shades can be raised up to the top of the window to allow the maximum view; yet, they can insulate as well as shade. Shutters and blinds offer mainly shade; for effective insulation, window coverings should fit tightly in the space, allowing little air movement behind and around them. Some windows actually come with integral shades inside two pieces of glazing. Since window coverings can be homemade, they are definitely cost-effective to install, for energy and privacy.

A wall of windows offers a lake view from the kitchen/dining area and a home office upstairs. (Architect: Richard Limmert; timber frame: Greg Merrill; owner/builder: Claire Miquet, Wakefield, Quebec, Canada.)

Trees shade the west windows in the late afternoon, reducing heat gain.

Landscaping to Enhance Comfort

Passive solar heat gain depends on having few obstructions to the southern sky. For passive cooling, you can utilize landscaping obstructions to your advantage. After considering your views, plant deciduous trees and/or vines on the west, east and/or south to shade your home during the hottest months. Since deciduous plants lose their leaves in the winter, the sun can still shine in when you need it most. Landscape or privacy walls can be quite effective as a windbreak, diverting chilly winds around your home, and creating a protected microclimate for plants and people in your own backyard.

What you learn about your climate and building site can pay off in an energy-wise house plan. Yes, it does cost more for extra insulation in ceilings and floors and for good-quality windows. But rather than buying expensive high-tech mechanical systems to insure comfort and footing increasingly higher energy bills, understanding and working with natural cycles will reward you with a cozy home that you can heat with a teakettle. You can choose to buy a "smart home," or to be a smart homeowner.

In a vast natural landscape, this adobe wall will create a beneficial micro-climate and protect landscaping from hungry wildlife. (Photo by Tom Bartels.)

Raising the top plate on a load-bearing straw bale wall. (Photo by Joe Kennedy.)

Structural Systems

STRAW IS WHAT IS LEFTOVER when grains—such as wheat, rice, oats, barley, rye, flax and triticale—are harvested. It has been used for millennia as fiber reinforcement for cob, adobe and straw-clay homes. In the 1870s, the horse-powered baling machine was invented, and it didn't take long for migrant workers to begin stacking bales for temporary homes. Modern baling machines pick up dry straw left in rows in the field, compressing them into rectangular blocks tied with either two or three wires, or polypropylene string.

The best bales imaginable would have long, uncrushed, dry straw, with 10 percent or less moisture content. They would be firm, dense and "square," with tight strings. They would be golden yellow and smell fresh. We sometimes have to settle for less-than-perfect bales, but do get the best ones you can, and avoid bales that are discolored or have high moisture content. Bales from any grain are suitable to build with, but for rot resistance, rice and flax bales rate the highest. Store them out of the weather or up on pallets under a tarp, and monitor your tarp if rain is expected.

The thermal resistance—or "R-value"—of straw bales is dependent on straw type, density, orientation and thickness. While 18-inch bales have measured as high as R-48 in some tests, the generally accepted rating for a stuccoed bale wall assembly is R-27, in a test performed by Oak Ridge National Laboratories in Tennessee. By comparison, the same lab rated a 6-inch frame wall filled with fiberglass (nominally R-19) at R-12.8.

Load-Bearing Walls

A major appeal of load-bearing, or "Nebraska-style," straw bale, is its structural simplicity: An energy-efficient wall system can be created with as few as two materials—plaster skins and a straw bale core. In fact, once plaster has been applied directly to the bale surfaces, the structure essentially becomes a stressed-skin panel. Effectively, any further "loading" (from snow, people, wind, earthquakes, etc.) will go mostly into the plaster skins, which are far stiffer than the straw. Creating this structural sandwich depends on plaster coatings being worked directly into the straw, as there is a huge increase in strength when they are well bonded to the bales.

A modest, single-story rectangular building lends itself to load-bearing design and will generally be cheaper to build than a post-and-beam-and-bale structure, primarily through reduced lumber costs. Load-bearing bale walls can generally be erected faster, too, as they avoid the inevitable interface with the structural system.

Load-bearing bale walls are stacked in a running bond with interlocking corners and tied together at the top of the wall with a top plate, or bond beam or "roof-bearing assembly." Roof rafters, or trusses, are attached to this rigid top plate which is tied to the foundation, typically with plastic or metal strapping. This serves to hold down the roof in a strong wind. The weight of the roof on top of the continuous bond beam should compress the bale walls evenly around the perimeter. The walls are allowed a month or so to settle under this weight—or are "pre-compressed" with various tensioning systems—before plaster is applied. Windows are installed in "rough bucks" which are inserted in bale walls as they go up. These wooden frames are cross-braced to stay square. They are held in place with dowels stuck through holes drilled in the sides of the frame and pounded into the bales. Window frames can be tricky to keep level as the bale walls grow: Be sure to check that they are "square" before tensioning down the roof. Generally, window and door bucks are later attached to the bale walls with metal or plastic lath to create a strong plaster connection.

A window "rough buck" is added to the straw bale wall.

Structural Skins

Plasters add structural strength to the wall—especially cement-based stuccos. In laboratory tests, compression strength, wind resistance, and racking sheer strength were significantly enhanced after cement/lime stucco was applied, irrespective of whether wire mesh was used. However, in seismically active California, a bale/stucco/wire-mesh struc-tural combination has been developed, which is showing great promise as a safe building system in an earthquake-prone area.

Through trial and error, bale builders have discovered ways to eliminate the onerous task of applying the standard stucco netting and expanded metal lath. It turns out that stucco and plaster stick quite well to the rough surface of a trimmed straw bale, and also "key in" to the joints between the bales, so mesh becomes optional—especially when the plaster is rich in chopped straw. Straw fiber serves to reinforce clay plasters—in the same way the addition of poly fibers reinforces cement stucco—and also reduces cracking. However, wherever bales abut a post or rough buck, the joint between them should be reinforced with a mesh. Expanded metal lath, stucco netting, plastic netting and burlap have all been used successfully, depending on choice of plasters. Whatever mesh is used, it should be secured across the crack and extend six or more inches onto the face of the bale.

Plaster Application

Cement or earthen plasters generally require a three-coat application. The first—a thick "scratch" coat—fills in major irregularities, and the second—a smooth coat—evens out the

A "weed-whacker" easily trims loose straw, creating a more uniform surface before plas-tering. These strawbale walls stacked "on edge" are stabi-lized with a set of bamboo poles—one on each side—tied tightly, like a corset.

Bales can be notched around posts, or the posts can be left exposed on the interior or exterior.

wall surface to the desired shape. The third coat, thinly troweled on, is a final color coat. Each coat should be fully dry before the next is applied. Cement stucco needs to stay moist for up to a week while it cures, or it will develop small cracks that are difficult to fill. Earth plasters will crack, too. Experiment with varying mixes of local clay and aggregate to see how they perform before committing to a recipe.

Post and Beam and Bale

A post-and-beam structure—with bales filling the walls for insulation—is generally required for larger, taller and more complicated floor plans. In this design, the roof loads are carried by the posts and beams. One big advantage of this method is that the roof can be finished before the bales are even delivered to the site. This provides a handy place to store bales out of the weather, and virtually guarantees there will be no wet bales.

The structural frame for an infill bale wall can be anything the local codes allow—wood, steel, concrete or adobe. It can go on the inside, outside, or be notched into the bales. Box columns and beams built from small dimensional lumber and plywood create a sturdy structure without the need to cut down big trees. Unmilled trees "in the round" can provide structure and display the beauty of a tree's natural shape. But working with round lumber requires greater skill than joining dimensional lumber.

Be sure to think through how your structure and bales will meet, as designing to minimize notching and custom bales will pay off in ease of construction.

Window and door framing is typically incorporated into the structural framework. Another advantage of post-and-beam building is the option of stacking the bales on edge, reducing the wall thickness (but not the effective R-value). However, on edge the strings are exposed to the wall surface, so notching bales for niches or to insert conduit is problematic. And since plaster doesn't stick as well to this slicker surface, plastering requires a bit more effort.

In both load-bearing and post-and-beam systems, it has been common for builders to pin bale walls through the center with rebar or bamboo. While this does help stabilize the wall during construction, it's now clear that such pins are no structural help once the plaster is applied. Stucco netting is also viewed as optional or is utilized selectively around door and window openings. Recent code revisions in California allow a "bed of nails" at the base of a wall to

A well-prepared bale wall is a pleasure to plaster, and good flashing details will pay off in the first hard rain. As with any home, poor detailing means more maintenance, or moisture problems can develop.

replace the rebar pins sticking from the foundations. It also grants a sizeable value (360 pounds per foot) to the strength of stucco against "racking sheer" forces, which eliminates the need for diagonal bracing in most designs for seismic areas.

Not all codes or code officials agree on what they will accept, so an important first step in the permit process is to initiate a dialogue with your local code department. In many jurisdictions, strawbale buildings are allowed under the "Alternative Materials and Methods" section, with the "stamp" of an architect or structural engineer. It is generally up to homeowners to document and defend their building choices. Fortunately, laboratory testing has satisfied code requirements all over North America, and these resources are available to aspiring bale builders.

Electrical wires can go right in the bales, though it's wise to limit plumbing in bale walls. To hang cabinets, a wood structure can be notched into the bales before plastering.

Straw bale walls infill a prefab steel framework. (Photo by Martin Hammer.)

Load-bearing versus Post-and-Beam

by Pete Gang, Architect

At this point in the evolution of strawbale building, if a strawbale structure is going to be engineered and permitted, the choice of load-bearing obligates one to use metal-mesh-reinforced Portland cement–based plaster, or stucco, which has a long list of despicable characteristics, including huge embodied energy, proclivity to cracking, and low vapor permeability, among others. The use of a post-and-beam (or non-load-bearing) structural system, on the other hand, disengages the important decisions of 1) structure and 2) plaster. In other words, in a post-and-beam structure, one is free to use any kind of plaster (earth, lime, gypsum, etc.) that is otherwise appropriate.

One important consideration in choosing plasters is the type and extent of lath or mesh needed for a given type of plaster. While stucco typically requires that the entire wall surface be covered with some kind of metal mesh (a significant undertaking in itself), an earthen plaster can be applied directly to the trimmed surface of the bales with quarter-inch burlap reinforcement applied only in certain specific places.

A final consideration in this decision is the matter of adaptability, or reuse. If we're designing decent buildings, they are destined to be added on to, remodeled, and messed with in all sorts of ways over their long lifetimes. Separation of skin and structure generally makes for easier additions and remodels, and therefore for more adaptable buildings.

Honest admission: In most cases, I favor a simple, wood-efficient post-and-beam structure with earthen plasters.

Small Is Beautiful

THINKING SMALL is a good way to begin any building project. Minimizing size also implies minimizing labor, materials and serious mistakes. From a simple shed to a guest cottage to a starter home that you can live in while you are building your dream home, starting small has many advantages—principally that your commitment of time and money can be reduced.

But don't think that because you're building half the size it will be half the cost. Fixed costs involving foundations and roofs, electricity and plumbing, and kitchens and bathrooms nearly always mean that smaller homes will cost more per square foot than bigger ones. Still, smaller generally means simpler, and simple bale buildings are especially appropriate for anyone building with bales for the first time.

A modest-sized rectangular bale building is great to learn and practice on. A load-bearing, shed-roofed, earth-plastered project is very forgiving, yet it can build your skills for taking on a larger structure. Keep it small enough and you may not even need a permit. Imagine a building you can do on weekends while holding down a regular job, or complete in a much shorter time span so you can move in sooner.

And be sure to plan for adding on later: Put in a door frame where a window will go or where you can build a future room. Or plan for several small buildings oriented together into a complex of living spaces. This allows you to live in a finished space rather than in a construction zone. In a mild climate, design to utilize outdoor space.

A bit of restraint will reduce your stress, unleash your creativity and help keep costs down. And you may find that a small house is big enough.

San Luis Obispo, California

After a raging forest fire had consumed their home near San Luis Obispo, California, architects Ken Haggard and Polly Cooper returned to the site to discover that two experimental stuccoed straw bale benches remained unharmed by the inferno. Appropriately, they decided to rebuild with bales, paving the way for straw-bale building in their county.

Before undertaking construction on their large home and office complex, they built a tiny, efficient cottage to live in on-site, which has now become a guest house for visitors and interns. The cottage provided a practical application for Ken and Polly, lovers of natural light and organic shapes, to try out design ideas as they explored this new medium of strawbale construction. Intentionally they sculpted bale walls into curvy shapes before plastering, thus creating a comfortable, curvaceous interior space with a whimsical exterior.

As pioneer straw builders, they chose a post-and-beam structure for ease of engineering. Friend and local builder Turko Semmes became their contractor, overseeing a wide variety of volunteers who turned out to help. Utilizing an existing slab, poles were set in concrete, and this structure was infilled with straw bales on edge. Bales were also used to insulate the fireproof metal roof. The cottage was finished with cement/lime stucco inside and out.

Building on a slope, the owners took great care to divert water around the structure. True south orientation combined with the thermal mass of the floor and plaster has eliminated the need for auxiliary heating in this coastal California climate. The cottage is also powered by photo-voltaic solar panels, so utilities are limited to gas consumed in cooking and showering.

Many of the trees killed in the fire were milled on-site, providing an abundance of wood for interior structure and trim. Ken and Polly were so inspired by building with straw bales that they have gone on to design many more homes and commercial structures using this "agricultural waste product." They find its superior insulation is the perfect fit with passive solar design, and they love the organic quality they can achieve. They advise, "Have fun! Curve the bales to your heart's content. And for small buildings, use bales on edge—proportions are much better."

Square footage: 450 interior, 500 exterior
1 bedroom, 1 bath, 1 story, post-and-beam
Architects: Ken Haggard, Polly Cooper, Scott Clark, San Luis
    Sustainability Group
Builder: Turko Semmes, Semmes & Co Builders
Strawbale Consultants: David Bainbridge, David Eisenberg
Approximate cost per square foot: $150

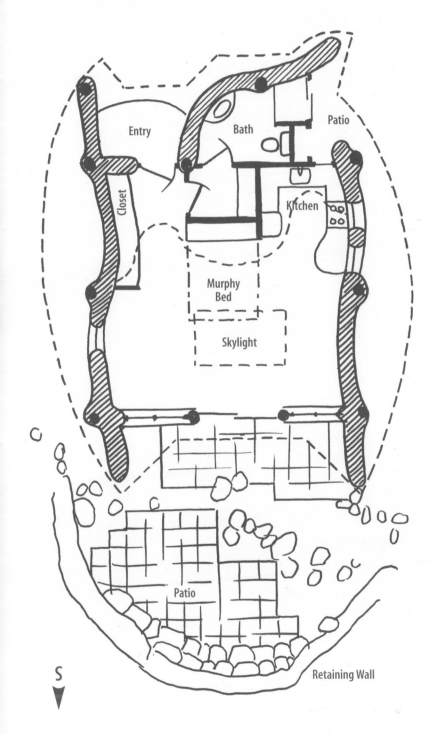

33

East Meredith, New York

In the rolling foothills of upstate New York, Astrid Nilssen built this modest home for herself and her two children based on a Norwegian-style house called a *jaarhus*. The style consists of a small two-story building with a gabled roof, with shed roof additions at either end. The upstairs contains two small bedrooms for the children, while downstairs are a kitchen/dining/living space and a larger bedroom. Its roughcast, thick, stuccoed walls are reminiscent of European building traditions.

Having a modest budget, Astrid chose to be an owner/builder. She was attracted to strawbale because "it makes a beautiful house," and as a non-carpenter, she was willing to attempt bale construction. She found it exciting to do something out of the ordinary, and benefited from having an experienced strawbale builder, Clark Sanders, as a neighbor.

The construction took eight months of full-time work with a paid carpenter. The result is a cozy and homey space, with every corner put to use. Windows orient to the south for solar gain, so Astrid burns only about three cords of wood per year. She has no reservations in advising others to just "do it!"

Square footage: 1,224 interior, 1,476 exterior
3 bedrooms, 1 bath, 1 ½ stories, post-and-beam
Owner-designed
Owner/builder (with help)
Strawbale consultant: Clark Sanders
Approximate cost per square foot: $45

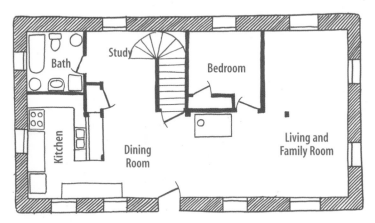

Bath

Study

Bedroom

Kitchen

Dining Room

Living and Family Room

Ground Level

S

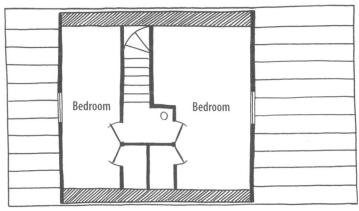

Upper Level

Bedroom

Bedroom

Solar gain is maximized on the south side with windows, a photo-voltaic solar panel and hot-water collectors that double as shade awnings.

FACING: A shapely juniper tree harvested from the house site, serves as a load-bearing post, as well as the center-piece to the room.

Crestone, Colorado

A contractor by trade, owner/builder Paul Koppana incorporated a host of ecological and budget-conscious ideas in his two-story home in Crestone, Colorado. This eclectic community boasts a plethora of alternative structures, benefiting from building codes that regulate only electrical and septic systems. Experimenting on his own home, Paul tried out a number of natural building techniques for cost-effectiveness and aesthetics, including earthen plasters, earthen floors and a hybrid structural system: a load-bearing second floor over a post-and-beam ground floor.

Bales were stacked "on edge," so their narrowest dimension (commonly 14 inches) makes up the wall thickness. While less stable going up, once plastered, this bale orientation has proven strong enough in historic load-bearing Nebraska homes to stand nearly a century, so far. Paul also pre-compressed the walls which actually makes them stronger, before adding earthen plasters on the outside and Structolite inside.

In siting his home, Paul considered the ease of creating a level site, solar orientation, and how few trees he would have to cut. One of these trees continues to live, used as the center support post inside the living room. Bales came from a reliable local farmer, Albert Francis, and Paul utilized local clay and aggregate for the earthen plasters, assisted by his experienced crew. Still, getting a durable plaster and earthen floor mix was a challenge.

An attached greenhouse doubles as a sun-filled dining space. With photovoltaic panels and solar hot-water collectors, Paul's combined utilities average around $25 a month. Paint (nontoxic, of course) was only used in the bathroom, mechanical room and on some doors. In retrospect, Paul would have added a small mudroom at the north entrance, for an air lock and a

place for visitors to remove their shoes. He also intends to close off the upstairs bedroom space for greater privacy.

As a homeowner, Paul is sold on strawbale for its great thermal performance, quietness, gently undulating walls and soft round corners.

Square footage: 1,000 interior, 1,200 exterior
2 bedrooms, 2 bath, 2 stories, post-and-beam/load-bearing hybrid
Architect: Touson Saryon, Integral Design Studio
Feng shui: Robin Cheri
Owner/builder: SkyHawk Construction
Earthen floors & plasters: Talmuth Mesenbrink, Jonathan Bruce
Solar systems: Randy Sizemore, Entropy Limited
Approximate cost per square foot: $95 (including solar systems)

Construction Details
• 24" wide by 30"-deep rubble-trench foundation, lined with landscape fabric
• 4" perforated pipe, with sock, in bottom of trench, with 1" to 2" washed rock fill
• 12" deep by 12 ½"-wide concrete grade beam on top of grade beam insulated with 1 ½" rigid foam
• First-floor post-and-beam structure with bales stacked "on edge."
• Second-floor load-bearing bales stacked "on edge." Between floors is a box beam or collar beam, 12" wide and 10½" high. Bales were pre-compressed.
• 3' eaves, except for the south, where 12" overhangs improve solar gain. Raised heel trusses give greater depth of insulation over the edge of the exterior wall.

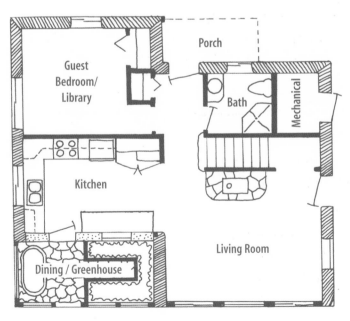

Ground Level

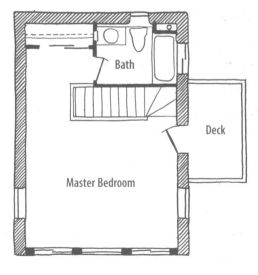

Upper Level

Whidbey Island, Washington
Maxwelton Creek Cohousing

A member of the Maxwelton Creek Cohousing community on Whidbey Island in Washington, Lea Kouba often hosts community meetings and parties in her spacious living/dining room. Visitors enjoy high windows on the south wall, which bring light into the core of the house and evoke the feeling of the white villages of the Mediterranean. A wraparound sunroom provides greenhouse space for starting seedlings and wintering-over plants. When the sun shines, the doors are opened to welcome the heat, but on rainy days doors are closed for comfort.

Lea's designer, Ted Butchart, chose Rastra, an insulated-concrete-form, to provide a well-insulated foundation that is vital in a cold climate. Radiant heat in a stained-concrete floor keeps the interior comfortable. The photovoltaic power system is inter-tied with Puget Sound Energy, providing enough power on sunny summer days to sell back to "the grid." The custom kitchen cabinets were built from recycled maple gym flooring and the stairs are made of local alder. Paints were avoided altogether inside, with non-toxic oils and stains used for wood finishes.

Members of Maxwelton Creek Cohousing, a six-home intentional community, affirmed low environmental impact as a top priority in construction. All home designs are compact and include solar orientation, recycled materials and maximum insulation. Lea went along with this consensus in choosing strawbale, and after living there, came to appreciate its warmth, flexibility and aesthetics. Her greatest challenge in acting as her own general contractor was her lack of building experience. And Lea's greatest joy in the process was the experience of community during the wall raising.

Square footage: 1,100 interior
2 bedrooms, 1 bath, 1 ½ stories, post-and-beam
Architect/strawbale builder: Ted Butchart
Framing and finishing: Frank Mesternacher
Approximate cost per square foot: $100

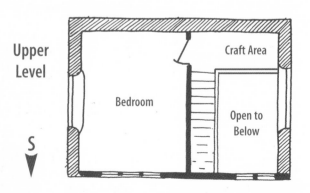

Upper Level

Bedroom

Craft Area

Open to Below

S

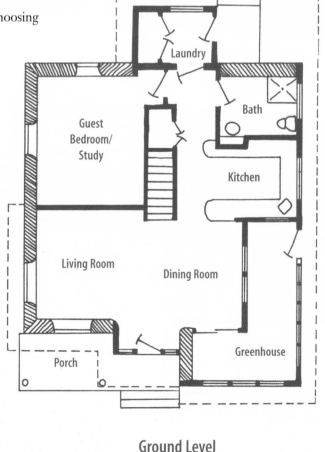

Laundry

Bath

Guest Bedroom/ Study

Kitchen

Living Room

Dining Room

Porch

Greenhouse

Ground Level

The south-facing front of this home is shaded by edible grape vines that help temper the climate inside.

A sunroom that wraps around the southeast corner of the house gathers heat and light and provides ventilation year-round. If the temperature is too warm or cold, the occupants can close it off from the main living space.

Charlemont, Massachusetts

Intrigued by the versatility and perceived ease of strawbale, landscape architect Andy Mueller opted to try it himself, after moving from California to Charlemont, Massachusetts. He chose a a hillside site for passive solar gain and mountain views, carefully considering drainage and integrating the home into an existing fallow orchard. The design for a high-tech loft in the woods with smooth timber-frame structure, industrial connections, and strictly straight walls, went through numerous permutations and continued to evolve during construction. The ultra-compact floor plan expanded as Andy, who now was engaged, visualized living in the space. The bath and utility room on the west grew in size, as did the loft space, with no real structural consequences. The wraparound porch was also an afterthought, so Andy had to notch bales to allow the beams through the walls. This notching allowed space for air to infiltrate the house, which had to be sealed with plaster.

Andy and his fiancée, Taya Rhodes, faced a number of challenges as owner/builders. They were not prepared for the amount of work this small building would take, especially with the fine finishing details they wanted; it took them a year to complete the building. But they moved into the building about four months into construction, right before winter. Their relationship was then put to the test as they lived for eight months in a construction zone.

Being a pioneer in the area, Andy had to have his post-and-beam design "stamped," or approved, by an architect, and he faced a conservative electrical inspector who required that the wiring be run through conduit. The cold New England climate required a four-foot-deep insulated frost wall. It was a challenge to keep tarps tight around their bales in the rain and wind, and to time the building process with the weather. They persevered, and the result is a stylish and functional home, built at about half the cost of a contractor-built home.

The floors are stained concrete, scored in large squares to resemble tile and sealed with a latex epoxy. Concrete with integral color was also used for the handsome kitchen countertops. The urban, industrial aesthetic is consistent with the streamlined use of space throughout. About a cord of wood per winter heats the space; backup electric wall-mount heaters have never been turned on. Andy and Taya applied an earth/lime/straw scratch coat, then successive coats of lime plaster inside and out, using burlap as reinforcement around doors and windows. Andy cautions that lime is very caustic, even when mixed with sand and clay.

He advocates using recyclable building materials. His favorite part was the collaborative process of meeting new people and hearing their ideas. Overall, Andy and Taya feel very proud of their home and the fact that they designed and built it themselves.

Square footage: 969 interior, 1,250 exterior
1 bedroom, 1 bath, 1 ½ stories, post-and-beam
Owner-designed
Strawbale consultant: Paul Lacinski
Owner/builder
Cost per square foot: $45

A wraparound porch offers inexpensive living space and an aesthetic front face. As the landscape matures, vines will add privacy and shade.

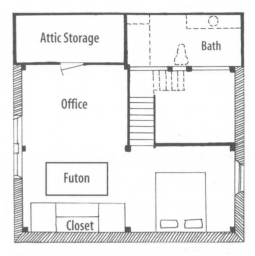

Attic Storage

Bath

Office

Futon

Closet

Upper Level

S

Ground Level

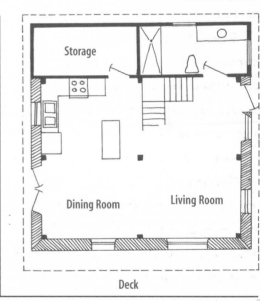

Storage

Dining Room

Living Room

Deck

ABOVE: A wraparound porch offers inexpensive living space and an aesthetic front face. As the landscape matures, vines will add privacy and shade.

BELOW: This contemporary style dictates precise plastering and metal brackets connecting the timber frame.

Urban Solutions

Iɴɪᴛɪᴀʟʟʏ, ꜱᴛʀᴀᴡ ʙᴀʟᴇꜱ don't seem suited to urban environments. Soft, squishy and organic, they seem out of place in the rectilinear world of steel and concrete, and the width of the bale wall may appear too costly where every square foot of space has a price tag.

But architects and builders are coming up with creative ways to utilize bales in the city. Efficient floor plans allow them to build on small lots, and with thoughtful designs they can easily fit strawbale to the neighborhood. The square footage "lost" to walls can be made up for by other qualities.

These thick, soft walls offer excellent sound dampening against noise disturbances like traffic, sirens and boom boxes. In multiple-family buildings, this sound insulation could allow increased density of neighborhoods by providing privacy now lacking. As thermal insulation, bale walls also offer increased comfort for less energy, pollution and cost. Nontoxic and cozy, they can also provide a healthy sanctuary from the urban jungle.

Still, city acceptance may not come easily. Code officials new to strawbale often resist it at first. A world apart from the materials they are familiar with, they worry about fire and other issues, and are concerned about their own liability. Fortunately, sufficient laboratory testing has been done to prove strawbale's stability and fire resistance, which can reassure code officials by answering their questions. This educational process usually becomes an additional task for the homeowner.

In the second-floor master bedroom, dormer windows create extra living space. Privacy and the amount of sunlight entering is controlled with insulating shades that both rise from the bottom and lower from the top. (Capitola, California)

There is also the challenge of changing perceptions. When a truckload of straw bales is being unloaded at your site, you will probably meet neighbors you've never spoken to before. To win acceptance from skeptical onlookers brainwashed by *The Three Little Pigs*, a friendly smile and a sense of humor are usually the best approach. You may even find them coming over to join the fun and lend a hand.

Berkeley, California

Owning a home in a noisy neighborhood in Berkeley, California, Nan Ayers and Eugene de Christopher dreamed about moving to the country. But the trade-off for peace and quiet would be a loss of convenience and a long commute. They decided instead to build a strawbale cottage in their own backyard.

Being the first strawbale pioneers in the city, they had the extra task of educating their code officials about building with bales. Fortunately, they found an experienced architect and engineer locally who could satisfy the strict requirements of building with bales in an earthquake zone. Of course, this seismic mitigation added to the cost of construction. Deciding to become their own contractors and do much of the work themselves helped reduce costs.

Still, they had a steep learning curve, and the project took about three years to complete. Nan and Eugene are quick to point out that they underestimated the skills required to build a home. The bale-wall raising was a joyous event, but only a minor part of the overall building process. Their inexperience caused things to take longer, as they had much to learn each step of the way.

They wanted a design that would be small yet comfortable, and leave them enough yard to create a lush landscape surrounding the home. The first floor is basically one room, with kitchen and living space defined by lighting, opening onto a spacious south-facing patio. This works as an intimate setting for entertaining. They chose a warm gray color for their stuccoed exterior and softer gypsum plasters inside, accented with strong colors for drapes and furnishings.

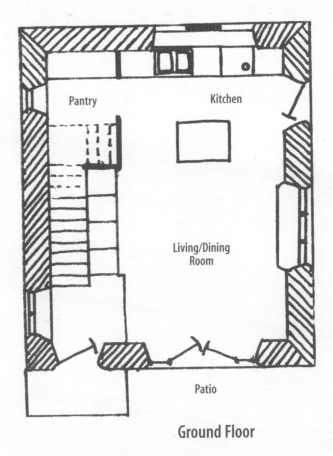

Ground Floor

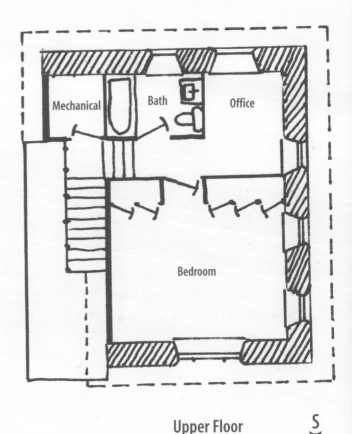

Upper Floor

S

In the summer, their west-facing skylight tends to overheat in the afternoon, but in winter, a single baseboard heater keeps the whole house comfortable. Their utilities are so low, in fact, that they thought their first bill was a mistake. While their greatest challenge was maintaining energy and enthusiasm over the long haul, Nan and Eugene love the soft edges and peaceful feeling of their urban sanctuary. And through his perseverance, Eugene gained confidence and new skills as a builder, and is now offering his services as a strawbale consultant.

Square footage: 898 interior
1 bedroom, 1 bath, 2 stories, post-and-beam
Architects: Dan Smith and Dietmar Lorenz, DSA Architects
Engineer: Bruce King
Owner/builder
Cost per square foot: $150

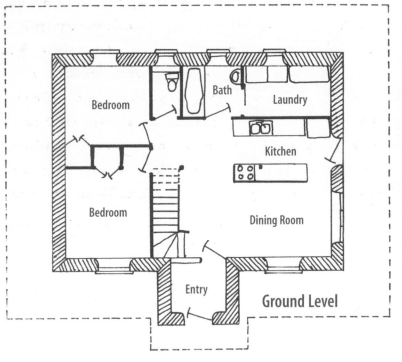

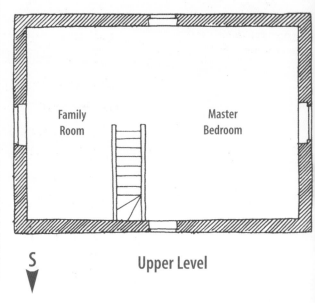

Bedroom

Bath

Laundry

Kitchen

Bedroom

Dining Room

Entry

Ground Level

S

Family Room

Master Bedroom

Upper Level

This colorful façade brightens the aging neighborhood of Aylmer, Quebec. The wide overhangs shelter against storms which swoop in off the Ottawa River.

Aylmer, Quebec

Kirk Finken and Danielle Roy saw their first strawbale building at a friend's party and fell in love with its warmth and its ecological and energy-efficiency aspects. They pushed through piles of red tape to build a load-bearing strawbale home in the town of Aylmer, near Ottawa, Quebec. The process even required the city to change its by-laws.

With plans of their own , Kirk and Danielle approached architect Linda Chapman, who prepared construction drawings and documents, and engineer Bob Platts, who created the structural design. Still, they went to four banks before finding a sympathetic loan officer who understood the engineering and health benefits of the building material.

Code restrictions were equally challenging. The city engineer made them jump through hoops, and skeptical inspectors devalued their work and ideas. But they retained their passion, stuck to their principles and won supporters. Finally the mayor came out in favor of strawbale as a new direction to take in ecological building, and Kirk and Danielle got their permit.

The first task was to take apart the old house on their lot, from which they salvaged and reused wood planking and paver blocks. Building load-bearing in this climate was challenging, as there is no roof during construction to protect bale walls from violent rains that blow in off the Ottawa River. (Kirk recommends getting a big tent to work under.) As much as possible, Kirk worked alongside the inexperienced subcontractors to keep things on track. Kirk and Danielle's favorite part of the process was getting dirty with family and friends during the wall-raising work party. Danielle particularly loved watching the plaster go on the bales—seeing the house take shape. After about four months, they moved in and threw a party for the volunteers. They extended the invitation to their local commissioners—and two of them came!

The design features three bedrooms with a large, open loft space for this family of four. The small entry vestibule acts as a mudroom and is essential in the winter for boots, coats, etc. Overhangs on the south are calculated for winter solar gain and also benefit from snow reflection, yet they amply shield the bale walls from the weather. An oil-burning furnace fuels radiant floor heat in the concrete slab for less than half the amount of the neighbors' heating bills.

Despite the challenges, Kirk and Danielle were empowered by their choice to build with bales. They advise, "Work with authorities as partners in change. Take a workshop, and get experience with the materials before you start on your own home." They found that collaborating with their architect and engineer was extremely positive. Most of all, they are very comfortable in their cozy strawbale. "Every time we pull up in front we think, 'That's a nice house!'"

Square footage: 1,500 interior, 1,800 exterior
3 bedrooms, 1 bath, 2 stories, load-bearing
Architect: Linda Chapman
Engineer: Bob Platts
Cost per square foot: $110 (Canadian)

Montreal, Quebec, Canada

A shade tree and a fence turn a tiny side yard into a sanctuary.

In dense downtown Montreal, Quebec, architect Julia Bourke created a compact strawbale design for her family of four on a shallow infill lot. She was attracted to the simplicity of the strawbale technique and wanted to expose people in the city to the idea of ecological housing in general. Naturally, the city of Montreal has various zoning and code restrictions, which required variances and engineering documentation. By utilizing the house as a demonstration project, she received a grant to pay for the urban analysis and city design part of the application.

Julia saved the trees on the tiny lot and created a side garden by positioning the house at the minimum setbacks on the south and east. She chose a slab-on-grade foundation for accessibility and thermal mass. The interior design seeks to eliminate hallways and utilize all the square footage. She's pleased with the floor plan but wishes it had more storage space.

Consulting with ecological-designer (and strawbale author) Michel Bergeron, they developed a "balloon-frame" structural system, using 2 x 4 lumber on eighteen-inch centers, and stacking bales vertically in between. The south wall is built with concrete blocks and windowsills for thermal mass. Custom cabinetry and baseboards utilize Isoboard, a strawboard made in Manitoba. For affordability, Julia chose standard windows and, with her husband, John, worked on the house herself: they had a fun-filled bale-building party and helped with the stuccowork and finishing, although they subcontracted most of the construction.

They used low VOC paints on doors and woodwork and milk paint to stain the exposed ceiling joists in the living room. Bales were plastered inside and out with a lime-rich stucco. To contribute to ongoing research, the slab and walls contain moisture monitors at each corner and every level. So far, the results are very encouraging. In this extreme northern climate,

Architect Julia Bourke designed a haven for her family, and an example of a different approach to infill housing, in the heart of Montreal.

Stained a light color, the exposed structural beams make the ceiling seem higher.

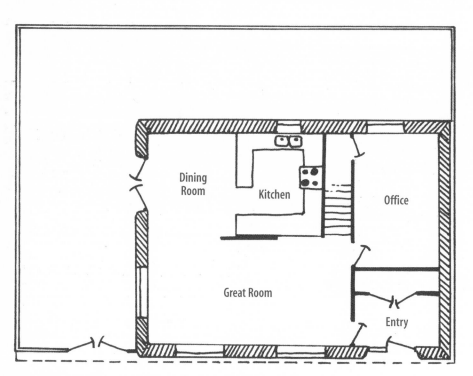

Dining Room

Kitchen

Office

Great Room

Entry

Ground Level

S

interior moisture condensation appeared only on the concrete-block walls, during rainy freeze/thaw weather. There is also some minor spalling of the exterior stucco toward the bottom of the concrete walls.

Julia cautions that "it's not as easy as the books make it seem." Still, she is encouraged by the flood of interest: in the week after completion, more than a thousand visitors toured their home. And she just plain loves the result. "It feels like a country house in the city," she says.

Square footage: 2,000 interior, 2,400 exterior
3 bedrooms, 2 ½ baths, 2 ½ stories, post-and-beam
Architects: Julia Bourke, Simon Jones, Emmanuelle Lapointe
Strawbale consultant: Michel Bergeron
Approximate cost per square foot: $150 (Canadian)

A bathtub rescued from the curbside is the centerpiece of this compact bathroom.

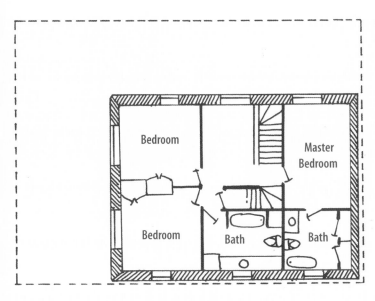

Upper Level

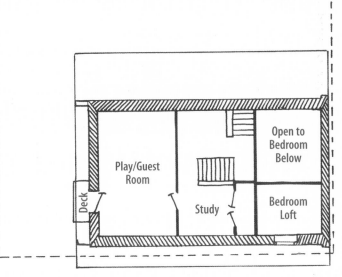

Attic

Flagstaff, Arizona

The weather in Flagstaff, which is surrounded by an alpine forest with an altitude above 7,000 feet, can rival the Rockies, so Cynthia McKinnon wanted an energy-efficient home. Utilizing a waste product appealed to her, and so did the aesthetic qualities of a bale wall juxtaposed with the geometry of windows and doors.

Despite hers being the first strawbale house in the city, her plans came back approved in ten days. Of course, Cynthia had done her homework. She had been gathering ideas, reading small-house design books and making sketches for years. The design should accommodate her family yet offer space for entertaining within a compact size. Consulting with the experienced strawbale builder Ed Dunn helped refine the floor plan and architectural details. Ed also drew the final plans for the post-and-beam-and-bale structure, which he submitted to the building code office, along with Tucson and New Mexico code guidelines. This reasonable approach, in a state fairly familiar with bale building, received a rapid positive response.

Cynthia had also been selecting the types of products she wanted to use in her house, including wool-fiber carpet and padding, formaldehyde-free wood, Saltillo tile sills and base-boards and a soapstone kitchen sink. Radiant-floor heating warms the scored-concrete floors, which are isolated from the freezing ground with an insulated-concrete-form (ICF) stem wall. With a bit of hindsight, she would separate her bedroom heating zone from the master bath zone so she could sleep in cooler temperatures and then step into a warm bathroom.

Passive solar orientation, double-paned windows and a well-insulated ceiling combine with the bale walls to produce heating bills one-third of that in the homes nearby. The handsome craftsman-style façade, complemented by a colorful drought-tolerant landscape, is an asset to the neighborhood. Cynthia confirms, "I am more pleased each day I live in this house."

Square footage: 1,850 interior, 2,160 exterior
3 bedrooms, 2 ½ baths, 2 stories, post-and-beam
Architect: owner-designed, consulted with designer/builder Ed Dunn
Builder: Ed Dunn, Solar Design and Construction
Custom carpentry: Brad Clark, Distinctive Woodworks
Approximate cost per square foot: $100

The craftsman-style façade and lush landscape of drought-tolerant native plants graces this suburban Flagstaff, Arizona, neighborhood.

Even with the more traditional separation of rooms, this compact design feels spacious because of the dramatic entry.

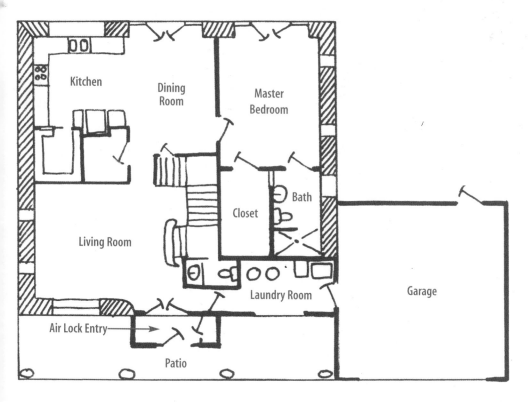

Kitchen

Dining Room

Master Bedroom

Bath

Closet

Living Room

Laundry Room

Garage

Air Lock Entry

Patio

Ground Level

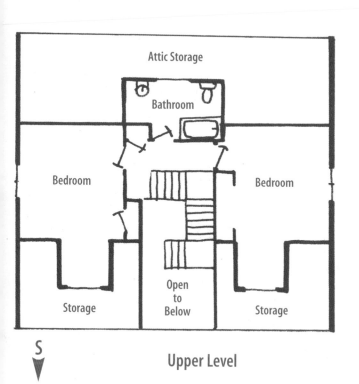

Attic Storage

Bathroom

Bedroom

Bedroom

Storage

Open to Below

Storage

S

Upper Level

The architectural lines in the bedroom are both clean and soft.

After ▲

The addition of a porch creates a shady outdoor room, and its ample overhang protects a wall of straw bales stacked around the outside. The bales were plastered with clay and decorated with a lime accent plaster.

Before ▶

Tucson, Arizona

After a decade of offering strawbale workshops across the country and around the world, strawbale pioneers and authors Matts Myhrman and Judy Knox faced a dilemma. A long-term tenant had moved out of their rental house, next door to their home in Tucson, Arizona. This modest concrete-block building was the kind of energy *in*efficient house they had been preaching against, and Matts and Judy decided they needed to do something about it—but what? Though its infrastructure was aging, the house was still substantially sound and too good to tear down. Finally, they decided to renovate it to increase its insulation against Tucson's intense summer heat by wrapping it with straw bales.

While the idea was simple, its realization was complex. Even in a desert, it does rain occasionally, so the roof would have to be extended to cover the additional thickness of the walls. And how would they insulate the roof to match the bale insulation? And how would they attach the bales to the existing structure and accommodate the existing venting and other services attached to the home's exterior? As they examined the possibilities, Matts and Judy gradually worked out answers to these and other questions.

First, the flat roof was insulated with 4 inches of rigid foam and blown-in cellulose and then painted with a reflective waterproof membrane to reduce radiant heat gain. The old single-pane windows were all replaced with argon gas-filled, double-paned, low-e windows.

Utilizing salvaged timbers, they built a wide portal structure along the south and east sides of the house covered with steel roofing. This wraparound porch adds a large amount of shaded outdoor living space, in addition to sheltering the new bale walls—and it looks nicer, too.

In spite of the shaded south porch, Matts and Judy still heat with the sun, thanks to a solar hot-air collector on the roof that bleeds solar-heated air in through evaporative cooler ducts. On the west side, the top of the strawbale wrap wall is

This concrete-block home in urban Tucson was an energy hog both in winter and in summer before undergoing a "bale wrap."

protected by a little steel rooflet built directly on top of the final course of bales.

Taking advantage of the construction process, Matts renovated the electrical service at the same time, sandwiching the new wires between bales and the block wall and adding custom-made outdoor fixtures to illuminate the portal. The bale walls were covered with earth during a well-attended plaster party, then accented with lime, thanks to help from a friend visiting from Germany. Finally a tall strawbale wall was built along the property line, creating an enclosed compound around their two houses, and the yard was transformed with a wheelchair-accessible permaculture landscape.

The process was not fast or cheap, but the results are nothing short of magical. Judy, who is now confined to a motorized wheelchair, can self-sufficiently scoot around the entire property, planting and harvesting vegetables, fruits, herbs and flowers.

Square footage: 900 exterior
2 bedrooms, 1 bath, 1 story, post-and-beam

Capitola, California

Kristin and Mark Sullivan's strawbale home in Capitola, California, is a fifteen-year dream come true. Their long-term vision was to build a solar, energy-efficient "green" home, and along the way the Sullivans discovered straw bales, a material that matched their ideals. Yet they wanted to build on an urban lot close to services, where they could walk, bike and roller-blade to the beach or a restaurant, and they had been warned that bales were too bulky for urban building.

Eventually they bought a small lot with a "tear-down" cottage on it. Their architect, Kelly Lerner, asked them to fill out a detailed questionnaire before she produced the initial design and floor plan. The final home is the result of a unique design collaboration between homeowners, architect and builders, who all worked "swimmingly" together. The nine-month construction process involved more than two hundred subcontractors, friends and family, who joined in on straw-bale and earth-plastering parties with a wonderful camaraderie.

The inviting craftsman face on this home conceals its self-sufficiency, which is cleverly integrated into the design. By siting the house at the minimum 5-foot setback along the north side of the narrow 45 x 100-foot lot, all the living space is oriented to the south for maximum daylight and solar heat in the winter. For summer and fall shading, deciduous grapevines will grow up on an arbor over the patio. Solar panels on the roof both heat water and produce electricity. Rainwater is collected and stored in a cistern to sustain the drought-tolerant edible landscape.

Inside, the open floor plan feels spacious, in large part due to the expanse of windows that extend the view. Built-in design features like arched doorways, a vaulted ceiling, *nichos* and wall "see-throughs" add elegance without clutter. Certain spots were designed specifically to display family heirlooms. Everywhere there is a consciously efficient use of space, exemplified by the compact staircase to the second floor, which functions also as a room divider and allows a shower to fit underneath. Amazingly, the first floor is also wheelchair friendly.

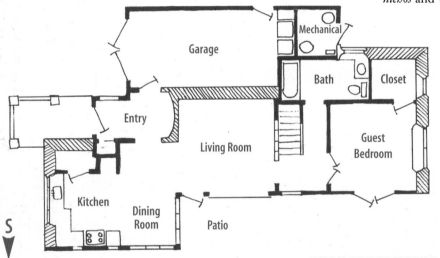

Ground Level

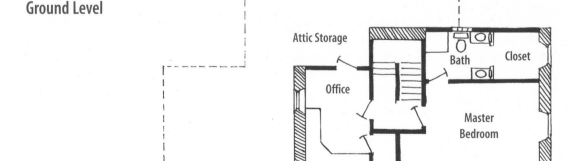

Upper Level

To maximize the south face, the Sullivan home is sited along the northern side of the lot, at the minimum allowed setback. The south-facing roof discretely holds both photo-voltaic and hot-water solar collectors. The Sullivans' combined electric and gas bill for July 2002 was under $8.

RIGHT: The floor plan was crafted with family heirlooms in mind. At the kitchen entry, this antique hall tree is both useful and handsome.

BELOW: By maximizing windows along the south, the long, narrow plan is flooded with light. The coastal climate is suited to indoor/outdoor living most of the year. Grapevines will grow fast to shade the patio during the hottest months.

Luscious, hand-applied earthen plasters of naturally occurring micaceous clay from New Mexico adorn the interior bale walls. Ferrous sulfate, a benign and inexpensive agricultural fertilizer, was used to stain the exterior lime/cement stucco. Other handcrafted details include built-in window seats, a recycled tile mosaic and the requisite truth window.

Consistent with the Sullivans' ecological goals, all of the wood used in construction was salvaged or sustainably harvested, including planking reused from the building torn down on the site. The stained- and scored-concrete floors utilize 30 percent fly ash, an industrial byproduct that reduces the use of cement. Blown-in cellulose, made from recycled newspaper, insulates the ceiling. The elegant front door was found at a salvage yard—a bargain at $150. But the antique sink in the downstairs bathroom cost as much, in the end, as a quality new one, given the cost of labor to replace the old fixtures.

Finally, Kristin and Mark installed energy-efficient lighting and appliances, including a "solar clothes dryer" (retractable clothesline). The cost of the photovoltaic solar system was reduced by half, thanks to California rebates, and being intertied to the grid eliminates the cost of batteries and allows power to flow in or out as needed. This translates to rock-bottom energy bills—their charge for electricity in July 2002 was 45 cents! Combined with gas and fixed costs, their total bill was under $8.

Ultimately, super-insulating straw bales became an essential element in this sustainable dream home, thanks to thoughtful design. The Sullivans' biggest challenges were balancing their ideals with budgetary concerns and finding the time to search out the most sustainable products. But they are proud of the fantastic educational opportunity their home has become for others, and they regularly allow guided tours for local college classes. Neighbors are proud, too, and seem to go out of their way to walk past this friendly façade.

Naturally occurring micaceous clay offers a creative opportunity for wall sculpture.

Square footage: 1,247 interior, 1,520 exterior, not including garage
2 bedrooms, 2 baths, 2 stories, post-and-beam
Architect: Kelly Lerner, One World Design
Builder: Michele Landegger and Debrae Lopes, Boa Constructor Building and Design
Solar systems: David Woodworth, Solar Vision
Approximate cost per square foot: $200

Los Osos, California

Retiring to California from Cleveland, Ohio, Jere and David Bresnan found a beautiful lot in a subdivision overlooking Morro Bay. Lovers of Santa Fe style, they had seen an article about strawbale in *Sunset* magazine and appreciated how it could emulate adobe walls. They also were impressed by its high insulation value. After additional research, they decided to build with straw and contacted the San Luis Sustainability Group to create plans for their home. But their idyllic site came with a number of challenges.

Their unique coastal ecosystem supports rare and endangered species, including the red-legged frog, banded snail, Morro Bay manzanita and ancient pygmy oaks—which it is illegal to disturb. The Bresnans' lot supports a lovely stand of 600- to 800-year-old pygmy oaks along its up-slope southern border, and down on the north is a drainage pond. With fifteen-foot setbacks to building from the property's edge, the home would have to fit inside a long, narrow strip on the bottom half of the lot. After several design iterations, it took nine months from submitting plans to getting a permit. This had less to do with strawbale, and more to do with convincing the Coastal Commission that their building would be sensitive to the natural setting around it.

A major benefit of building on the east/west axis is the view to the north, where the constantly changing weather over Morro Bay can be appreciated from every room. The shade of the hill and oak grove compromised passive solar opportunities, which were made up for by allowing in heat and natural light from thirteen skylights. (The cloudy coastal climate prevents summertime overheating.) A private wheelchair-accessible wing was designed on the east to accommodate David's mother, and a separate suite at the west end houses their college-age son. David and Jere enjoy a master bedroom on the second floor, where they've also installed a complete darkroom for Jere's photography.

FACING: Since the bay view is to the north, architects utilized thirteen skylights to bring natural light into the living space. The whimsical forms of the doorway and walls mimic the sculpted quality of the bales.

The Bresnans had never built a home before and were challenged by the thousands of decisions they had to make during the process. But they felt that building with bales was not any more difficult than building a regular house—it might even be a little easier, and it was fun to do. The architects helped organize the wall-raising party, bringing thirty-five students and architects from nearby Cal Poly University, and most of the walls went up in a single weekend. (Bales were not used for the north window walls or the second floor.) Their straw bales came from the Sacramento Valley, where the annual burning of the rice fields (now limited by law) used to create a huge air pollution problem.

The Bresnans' large, complex home took eleven months

The buildable area of the lot was a narrow strip between a drainage pond on the downhill side and a grove of rare, endangered pygmy oaks to the south, along the street access.

to complete, and includes custom-made tile, light fixtures, and carved cabinets and front door. Their builder found it difficult to route plumbing outside of the bale walls, and the skylights were tricky. Still, Jere and David love their home, nestled between ancient oaks and the deep blue sea, "and so does everybody else. It's so quiet," they remark, "that to listen to the ocean, we have to open a window!"

Square footage: 3,525 interior, 3,658 exterior
5 bedrooms, 4 baths, 2 stories, post-and-beam
Architects: Ken Haggard, Polly Cooper, Scott Clark, San Luis
Sustainability Group
Builder: Bruce Robertson
Approximate cost per square foot: $140

Upper Level

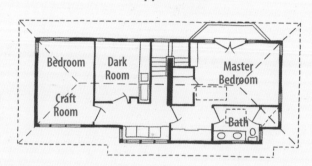

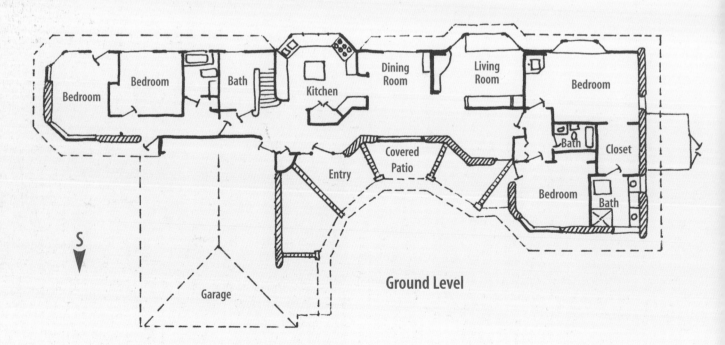

Ground Level

A spectacular view of Morro Bay was the reward for attempting the challenge of building a home on a sensitive, restrictive infill lot.

The wonderful view of Morro Rock makes time spent in the kitchen a pleasure.
RIGHT: The Bresnans' truth window.

Multitasking Environments

SOMETIMES A HOME needs to be more than just a comfortable place for one family to live.

A home can also be a workspace, doubling the use of common rooms and utilities. Living and working at the same location requires discipline but eliminates the chore of a commute. Connected private units or even separate small buildings grouped together can be a way to increase the versatility of space. And the addition of a home office or workshop wired for the Internet can make telecommuting a practical choice. It may even save your sanity.

Your dream home can be designed to evolve as your life changes: children grow up; parents come back to live with you. What about accessibility? Wide zero-step doorways cost a fraction to install during construction compared with retrofitting later. And it feels good to be able to welcome in wheelchairs without worrying.

Your home also contributes to your financial security. In fact, it's probably the biggest investment you'll ever make, so maximize its value. A rental unit can reduce the cost of your mortgage, especially in urban areas where decent affordable housing is scarce. And having a close neighbor who is also a friend is a benefit money can't buy.

The life of your home can be a hundred years or longer. It should keep doing the work you designed it to do long after you've left the planet. So why not choose quality? A well-built home is a wise use of resources, and chances are your efforts will be appreciated for generations to come.

By utilizing recycled building materials, taking his time and doing it himself, resourceful owner/builder Bill Ellzey kept his per-foot cost way down.

Crestone, Colorado

When professional photographer and world traveler Bill Ellzey bought a piece of rangeland near Crestone, Colorado, his primary goal in building was to take advantage of the spectacular views of the Sangre de Cristo Mountains to the northeast (no matter that this compromised passive solar orientation). Being a handy, self-reliant, confirmed bachelor, Bill set out to build his home his own way.

Crestone is well known as a community of free thinkers and a hotbed of strawbale and alternative building, so Bill fit right in. In this county, code requirements are minimal, and the community of builders and owner/builders were supportive and willing to share information. He began collecting salvaged materials to use in his home, including four 5 x 8-foot double-paned, tempered-glass windows that were being thrown away in a bank remodel in Boulder. These became the view windows facing the mountains, and other windows were donated by friends. Having the windows first, Bill designed his house around them.

He chose a simple rectangle with a shed roof for ease of construction. Inside he needed the usual spaces—kitchen, bedroom, bath, etc.—plus room to process, mount, mat and store his archives and growing collection of photographic images. As the building took shape, he found he loved the openness of the one big room, so the only partition walls that go all the way to the ceiling are around three clustered rooms—the master bath, guest bath and utility room. While Bill is 100 percent satisfied with this arrangement, he admits that "now I have a sweetheart who wishes we had one room as an 'away room,' a place for quiet contemplation or radio or TV listening/watching that could be closed off from the main part of the house."

Bill designed the house during the winter of 1995, began the foundation in April of 1996, and hosted Thanksgiving dinner for fourteen in a mostly completed house in 1999. He chose cotton batt insulation above the ceiling, with a steel shed roof over tarpaper over plywood sheathing. He bought local wheat straw bales and chose not to use stucco netting before applying cement/lime stucco inside and out. Kitchen, bath and utility floors are of durable concrete, while Bill preferred an earthen floor for his other living spaces.

A propane-powered radiant-floor-heating system keeps the space cozy for an average of about $50 per month, including heat, domestic hot water and cooking. Bill is quite pleased with this, noting, "I have huge windows facing the northeast mountains, so I'm sure I lose heat through them in winter."

Bill found his greatest challenges were the harsh Crestone winters, and "paying off the friends who loaned the money." Still, in doing the work himself, he created a comfortable home for a rock-bottom price. "I wouldn't change a thing," he claims, and adds, "Bales are relatively easy to work with. It was nice to know that I was using replenishable material that would otherwise have been plowed under or burned off. Also, I was anticipating a warm, quiet house."

Square footage: 1,440 interior, 1,792 exterior
1 bedroom, 1 ½ baths, 1 story, post-and-beam
Architect: Owner-designed
Owner/builder
Bale broker: Albert Francis
Approximate cost per square foot: $22

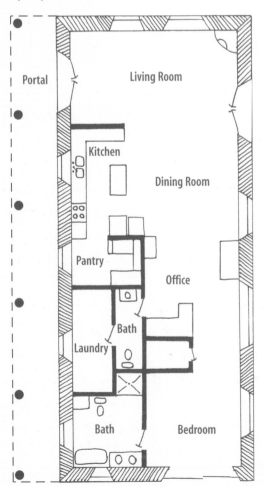

Patio

Advice From Owner/Builder Bill Ellzey

I had never done framing work, but I had stacked more hay in my youth than I care to remember. After seeing *The Straw Bale House,* I was convinced that a sound house could be built with this material.

Since Crestone is a hotbed of strawbale building, it was easy to go around to other sites and chat up the builders. Many said, "This is how I did this, but if I were doing it again I'd do such and such." That's invaluable to a wide-eyed novice. I built about 99 percent of my house. The other help came from neighbors and friends, some of whom were building at the same time. When something was too heavy to lift or set in place, we helped each other. I got the basics of plumbing and electrical wiring from books and a little manual called *Code Check.*

For simplicity of plumbing installation, I routed it down one side of the house only. I drew up a plan and ran it by the local plumbing shop. Anyone should be able to make a drain slope downhill, but doing it to code is another matter. The plumbers were eager to help. I went back and made sure I could get a wrench on every union and fitting that has threads, in case I need to do some maintenance.

My electrical design included dedicated circuits for computer equipment, more than enough outlets inside the house, plus outlets on the outside, and switches in the house for the barn light. For wiring the electrical to code, I consulted with the local electrician's son. He was interested in photography, which is my profession, so we did some trading. I hate to redo anything so I made pretty sure I had it right before calling for the state inspections. It's even worth paying a plumber and electrician to come by and check out what you've done before gluing up fittings or finalizing the wiring.

Probably the most unique features of this house are the window and door reveals. I built columns for the posts that support the box beams, and they also frame each window and door. Their cross section is a right triangle. The bales butt against the 90-degree side, while the angled side (hypotenuse) becomes a "beveled" side of the window opening. Same for the doorways, except that the doors are set on the inside plane of the bale walls while the windows are set on the outside plane. So the window openings get larger to the inside of the house and doorways get larger to the outside.

Taos, New Mexico

As they discussed what their new home would look like, Martie Moreno and Roger Johnson kept returning to the Overland Sheepskin Company in nearby Taos, New Mexico. The weathered log ceilings, dormer windows and rustic, hand-hewn finishes matched Martie's vision of her perfect weaving studio. Finally, they said to each other, "Let's just build this." So they did—and then some.

Martie had already been to a friend's strawbale wall raising and had fallen in love with the material and the process. She also loved the deep windowsills and appreciated straw's natural, nontoxic nature. Their architect, Karlis Viceps, suggested several integrated passive and active solar design ideas. The result is a nearly self-sufficient home that uses strawbale upstairs and pumicecrete downstairs.

From the day they bought the land, Martie and Roger planned their two-story home for solar gain. The south-facing first floor receives direct gain through thermopane windows and indirect gain through 8-inch-thick concrete "Trombe walls." (East, west and north ground-floor walls are sixteen-inch, poured-in-place pumicecrete.) The glass-faced Trombe walls absorb heat on sunny winter days and radiate that warmth into the home—what Karlis calls the "heat-generating zone." A low adobe wall that creates the bedroom space does double duty as a heat sink for sunlight streaming in the southern windows. At high elevations in northern New Mexico, the winter nights are cold, but on most days the south wall receives six hours of sunlight, which "charges up" the pumice-and-adobe thermal-mass walls and keeps interior temperatures comfortable. Martie's cats don't

Ground Level

Shower

Pantry

Laundry/ Storage

Storage

Mudroom

Living Room

Bath

Bedroom

Kitchen

Dining Room

S

Trombe Wall

In areas where forest fires are a danger, homeowners are advised to clear flammable vegetation from within thirty feet of the house.

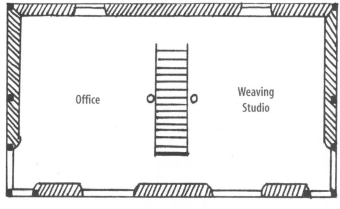

Upper Level

Office

Weaving Studio

understand the theory but get the results: they're frequently found on the window walls soaking up sun.

A rustic portal protects the north-facing front door, which opens into an air-lock mudroom. The low ceilings in the living/dining area open up into a light-filled country kitchen. Upstairs is Martie's weaving studio—one big, open room filled with a loom and a rainbow of yarn. Roger's computer is tucked into a corner nook. The ceiling *vigas* (log beams) were harvested "standing dead" and used with the bark intact. The strawbale walls upstairs are finished with aliz, a lustrous clay finish plaster created by Taos resident Carole Crews. Downstairs floors are stained, acid-etched concrete. Upstairs floors are rustic pine boards.

Roger's work as an engineer often keeps him on the West Coast, so Martie supervised the eleven months of construction. Their biggest challenge was planning the various energy systems for self-sufficiency, so they had backups for everything. The radiant floor heat and the solar batch heater that provides domestic hot water are backed up with a gas-fired hot water heater (CombiCor). The well serves as backup for their rainwater catchment system. Thanks to their 2-kilowatt photovoltaic system, Martie and Roger paid no electrical utilities until the noise of their generator motivated them to tie into "the grid" to charge the batteries when necessary. Now they're paying only the $10 monthly charge.

In hindsight, Martie would do some things differently. "I would prefer more space to our country kitchen, where I spend most of my time. I find the extra space in the bedroom isn't important, as I spend so little time there. Also, the sound

Open shelving displays collectibles and keeps dishes close at hand in this functional country kitchen.

carries in the open floor plan and through the wooden floors." Still, Martie is pleased to be surrounded by straw in her light-filled weaving studio. "I love our strawbale walls and the sensuous way they undulate, in contrast to the flat predictability of drywall or pumice walls," she says.

Square footage: 2,622 interior, 3,024 exterior
2 bedrooms, 2 baths, 2 stories; post-and-beam
Architect: Karlis Viceps, Energyscapes
Builder: John Hunt, Alternative Home Builders
Pumicecrete: Beau Schoen, Schoen Construction
Custom kitchen/front door: Glenn Sweet
Earthen plasters: Carole Crews, Gourmet Adobe
Solar system: Paul Arvila, Ute Mountain Electric
Approximate cost per square foot: $125 (including solar system)

Light and view enhance the bathing experience in this antique tub. Barely visible are wires from moisture monitoring probes, left in the bale wall so the owners can periodically check the humidity in the straw.

Working with Subcontractors

Martie Moreno

Here are a few suggestions for happy results, based on my experiences:

Keep a file of design ideas, furniture ideas, storage, finishing details, paint, etc.—magazine clippings work great. It's better to have too many than not enough. Use them to convey your ideas to those involved in the building process. It helps them to know what you are envisioning. Pictures do speak louder than words.

I found it advantageous to be on the job frequently. Don't disrupt the work, but set a point each day to discuss things with the contractor or person in charge. I made daily lists and copied them so we could go over things and both have something to remember our discussion by.

On being a woman working with tradesmen, hold your ground! You may hear this phrase in various forms: "Let me tell you what you want." Ask lots of questions. Don't be timid about trying to find a solution to a design challenge just because you've never built a home before. Compromises made in haste may leave you unhappy for a long time. It's your home and you are paying for it.

When it comes to special architectural pieces—hardware, sinks, tubs, whatever—it's best if you have them to incorporate into the planning process versus adding them during construction.

Upstairs, south-facing and view windows bring natural light into this weaver's studio.

A prefabricated steel frame wrapped with bales provides a cost-effective structural system for a large, open space. While the skeleton is a rectangle, the front is curved for a softer façade.

Annapolis, California

Chris Poehlmann designs and builds interactive museum exhibits for a living. It's his business to create attractive, functional exhibits by combining materials in unexpected ways. When he turned his attention to building his own workshop among the majestic coastal redwoods in northern California, of course he thought "outside the box."

He and his partner, Janice Bonora, wanted to build with straw bales for their sustainability and energy efficiency, but their land in Annapolis, California, is near the San Andreas Fault, so they needed a sturdy post-and-beam structure. With 101 inches of rain a year, a good roof and large overhangs were also important. He needed what he called "big dumb space" to construct his museum projects, but they also wanted a studio space in the same structure. Ultimately, Chris and his architect fused industrial steel and low-tech straw bales in an innovative design that addresses all these concerns.

Chris ordered a modular prefabricated metal storage building—without the metal siding. It was delivered ready to assemble with plans and factory support. This provided an industrial-strength metal roof and a strong steel framework with a vaulted clear-span truss system, which maximizes usable interior space. He poured a concrete slab and precisely positioned the bolts that connect the steel frame to the slab. Once the slab had cured, Chris erected the steel framework in two days, with a little help from his friends and a crane to lift the steel trusses into position. Then they brought in the straw bales and stacked them to create a curved front wall well inside the steel frame to allow the metal roof to act as a generous overhang. Chris invented his own tools to sculpt the bales, including a Sawzall fitted with the blade from an electric carving knife, and a roto-hammer to drive in the rebar pins. He wrapped the bales of the south-facing wall in "housewrap" to protect them from wind-driven rain.

One of the biggest challenges was creating a curved top plate to tie the front wall into the steel structure. His architect's solution was a curved plywood box beam stuffed

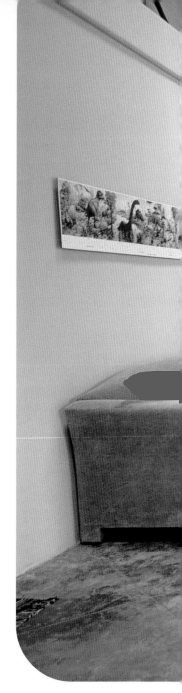

with straw that was built in place. Chris plastered the bales with cement stucco and used what was left over to finish surfaces in the bathroom. Lumber milled from fallen pine trees next to the house was used for ceilings.

The front section of the structure is a cozy art studio, which features *nichos*, a plastered strawbale bench, a wood-burning stove and a sculpted oval truth window. An office loft overlooks the shop space that occupies the back two-thirds of the 3,680-square-foot building.

Chris is a professional craftsman and general contractor with a master's knowledge of tools and techniques. Although he did much of the work himself, he also had help from friends, including his architect, Martin Hammer. Although the bale walls and their plastering can utilize unskilled labor, Chris advises that "building with bales doesn't necessarily make the construction process any easier. It requires expertise. At some point, you'll need expert help."

Square footage: 3,180 interior, 3,680 exterior
Shop (2,160), office loft (505), art studio (1,015); post-and-beam
Architect: Martin Hammer
Owner/builder
Steel framework: Web Steel, Sandy, OR
Approximate cost per square foot: $34
 Note that recycled and free materials were used where possible,
 including interior doors, lights, and plumbing fixtures.
 Costs shown are for building materials only.

Office (above Bedroom & Studio)

Under-Roof Storage

Bedroom

Lounge

Bath

Workshop

Studio

S

ABOVE: In the studio, the curved bale walls create a comfortable space to relax in.

RIGHT: The tall steel trusses create a large, useful workshop space for a modest per-square-foot cost.

Tucson, Arizona

After an amicable divorce, Caroline Coalter Wilson took her settlement and used it as seed money to build a home of her own—a strawbale home. This is not so remarkable in Pima County, Arizona, where strawbale is well known and has been part of the codes since 1994. But instead of the house being an economic burden, Caroline made it work for her, and here's how.

By riding her bicycle around her rural neighborhood west of Tucson, she made a list of vacant lots with views she liked, and contacted the owners to see if they might be interested in selling. Only two responded, but one was enough, and they both saved by making a deal without a realtor involved. Next, Caroline drew up her own design, hiring an architect to check over her plans and help with technical drawings. She also found a builder, Jon Ruez, who specializes in assisting owner/builders with strawbale construction. "He was very helpful every step of the way," raves Caroline.

In siting her home, she thought about south-facing windows for solar gain, the beautiful views to the west, positioning the house so it was screened from the road, and drainage. The single-story pueblo-style building and the surrounding strawbale garden walls maintain a low profile and fit organically into the desert landscape. "I love the look of strawbale buildings, their thick walls, deep windowsills and the ability to have window seats and *nichos*. Plus, I wanted the insulative qualities afforded by strawbale."

Following a year from conception to ground breaking, the construction took about nine months, with Caroline acting as the general contractor, aided by her experienced builder. They incorporated typical energy-efficient features, including R-38 ceiling insulation, a reflective metal roof, double-paned wood windows, and an evaporative swamp cooler that works well in the dry climate with a minimum of power consumption. Caroline is very satisfied, "My utility bills are lower in this house than in any other of my living situations."

They also created a water-harvesting system that collects rainwater from the roof in an underground concrete tank for use in watering the garden and native landscape. The plumbing system utilizes pex-type tubing, with an easy-access manifold to distribute it throughout the home. This eliminates all connections in-between the manifold and the fixture, for a low-maintenance system.

Not surprisingly, Caroline found the best part of building with bales was the wall raising, "It was so much fun to have my friends come and help build the walls of my house." Her biggest concern was "money! And worrying if my design was going to come out right."

In the Sonoran desert near Tucson, Arizona, this low pueblo-style profile fits into the landscape, and its wraparound straw-bale wall keeps out crawling critters without blocking the view.

The main part of the house is a one-room cabin concept, with cooking in one corner, a private sleeping nook in another, the bath in another and living room in the other, with the dining area in the middle. Caroline intended the modest guest wing to accommodate visiting friends, but nobody was coming to visit, and she thought, "What a waste." Then, "about the sixth time I wrote out the mortgage check and noticed what a big chunk of my paycheck that was, it occurred to me that perhaps the house could help pay for itself. I didn't want to have a roommate, and hit on the idea of turning my guest room into a bed and breakfast," she said, and thus Paca de Paja (meaning "bale of straw") B&B was born.

Keeping her day job at Tucson's Desert Museum, she has calls forwarded to her cell phone so she's always available to take reservations. With a single suite to book, her host duties are manageable and she's not busy every night. Being a gregarious person, Caroline finds this sideline brings an interesting dimension to her social life: "I love it! The B&B is a fun thing to do, and it's great to share information about strawbale building with my guests. I recently had a young Russian couple stay with me—it's like traveling without leaving my living room."

Square footage: 1,278 interior,
    1,656 exterior
2 bedrooms, 2 baths, post-and-beam
Architect: Owner-designed,
    consulted with architect
Builder: Jon Ruez
Approximate cost per square
    foot: $83

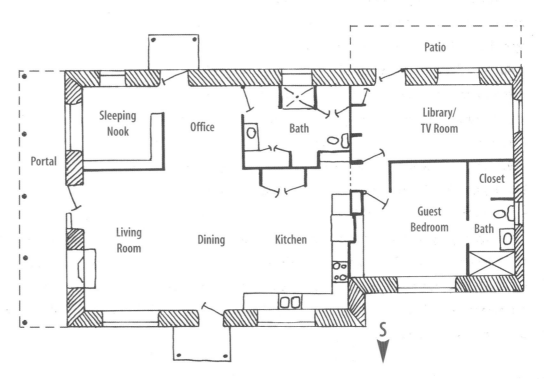

Kingston, New Mexico

In the foothills of the Gila National Forest in southern New Mexico is a small town called Kingston, where I (the author) live and run the Black Range Lodge. Built of brick, stone and logs in the 1880s and the 1930s, the doorways are narrow and floor levels change abruptly; all the guest rooms are on the second floor. It has a lot of character but isn't accessible for my father, who gets around in a motorized wheelchair. Eventually, we decided to build an accessible strawbale guest house just up the hill from the lodge, for when my parents visit.

To disturb the landscape as little as possible, we utilized an existing clearing and dug into the hillside to create a split-level structure. The top level has its own driveway, and decks stick out of the hillside to take advantage of a wide view of the mountains from east to west. The downstairs is like a day-lit basement: on the south is a retaining wall against the hill, and windows open to the east, west and north. This downstairs is divided between a workshop/mechanical room and a studio apartment. Upstairs is a spacious one-bedroom home, built expressly to be wheelchair friendly.

The design evolved from the site, a 30 percent slope. We decided to connect the upstairs and downstairs via concrete stairs around the outside to save room on the inside. The result is two separate, versatile spaces: a downstairs studio apartment for visiting family and friends (or potentially, a caregiver) and an upstairs that meets my parents' needs. And when my parents aren't visiting, we can rent the spaces out as an adjunct to our bed and breakfast.

To create the post-and-beam structure, we used rough-cut dimensional lumber wherever it would be hidden in the wall, and ponderosa pine logs for the structure wherever it was practical to expose it. The logs were hand-peeled and lightly sanded to retain the character of the individual trees. We harvested them sustainably ourselves, with a $30 permit from the forest service—they were mostly smaller trees, taken from a stand of pines that needed thinning.

Living in an urban area, my mother shopped for salvaged windows, fixtures, sinks, etc. Some pieces turned out to be quality bargains, but things like sinks and toilets cost as much to restore as it does to buy them new (if character doesn't play into your choice). She also colored the concrete floors herself with multiple applications of ferrous sulfate, an inexpensive fertilizer that stains cement a coppery color. The floors turned out looking like shiny leather.

Imbedded inside is a continuous loop of pex tubing that circulates hot water through the insulated concrete slab for radiant heat. Because radiant heat doesn't work fast, an airtight woodstove quickly takes the

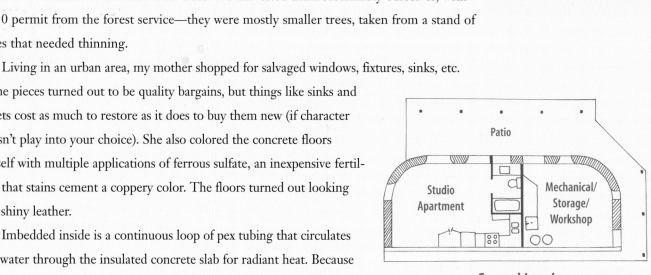

Ground Level

Carved into a hillside on a small lot, this home is sited to take advantage of views in all directions.

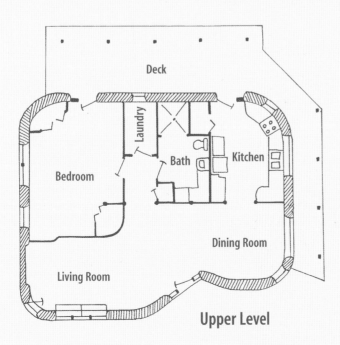

Deck

Laundry

Bedroom

Bath

Kitchen

Dining Room

Living Room

S

Upper Level

chill off the space when necessary. Our mountain climate and passive cooling strategies mean that the strawbale house doesn't need a cooling system, so there is no forced-air ductwork anywhere in the house. And when my father comes to visit, guess what? His dust allergies go away.

Throughout the home we wanted to demonstrate the sculptural qualities of the walls. Although the structure is rectilinear, the walls curve around to create an intimate oval shape to the dining and living rooms. Decorative *nichos* and a truth window are carved into the surface of the bales, and the final finish is a polished aliz. With tiny bits of straw and mica in the mix, the surface has texture, and it sparkles subtly throughout the day as the light moves across it.

But my favorite part is actually watching the light move across the landscape, from inside. A large picture window frames a killer view, and the space feels warm and intimate, as well as connected with the natural world. We are proud to share with visitors our version of a strawbale dream house, and love it even more when we get to share time there with my parents, Ralph and Betty.

Square footage: 1,752 interior, 1,912 exterior
2 bedrooms, 2 baths, 2 stories, post-and-beam
Owner-designed, with consulting architect Bill Buckley
Builder: Tom Lander
Aliz plaster: Carole Crews, Gourmet Adobe
Custom woodwork: Bill Kernan
Estimated cost per square foot: $100

LEFT: A studio apartment on the lower level has its own private patio.

BELOW: The curved interior walls, finished with an earthen aliz plaster, give an intimacy to the large space. A stained concrete floor and the open floor plan allow easy wheelchair access throughout.

Question and Answer with Betty Wanek

Why did you decide to build with straw bales?

I was intrigued by the concept. It seemed to have all positives, not only as a building material but also as a sensible, simple and easy way to help save our trees while providing farmers with a cash crop.

How do you feel about the final result?

It is actually better than I had anticipated.

Are you pleased with your floor plan? Would you change anything about it?

Yes. It is an open floor plan, designed for easy access inside and out for a handicapped person in a wheelchair or scooter. I would probably change the truss design to create more headroom, and allow the big attic space to be more useful for storage.

Who did you consult with in your design, and what building professionals helped in the construction?

The final design was my own, but it was a product of many suggestions by many people . . . people from whom I had asked for input. It progressed from a simple, very small weekend cottage to a complicated two-story, then back to a simple design, still taking advantage of the hillside site. Major credit goes to my builder Tom Lander for his craftsmanship, start-to-finish. My son Richard and son-in-law Pete also helped with a number of tasks, from harvesting the trees and excavation, to tiling and painting.

When did you begin the design phase? The construction phase? Move in?

The summer of 1995. Early '96. July '98.

What was the best part of the process of building with straw bales?

The fun of seeing a gang of people all helping out—some hired, some volunteers—and working with them. Plastering with natural plaster, stuccoing, hauling bales, the camaraderie of it all.

What were the greatest challenges and concerns during the building process?

Adhering to the plans, having workers when needed, my personal concern of not being able to be on-site at all times when work was progressing—a "must" for an owner, in my opinion. One should be on-site with drawing in hand, with measuring tape and level at the ready.

What other special details did you incorporate?

The home is designed for handicapped accessibility, with all doors 36 inches wide and all floors at the same level, hard and smooth. The deck is wide and wraps around the whole top floor. The bathroom has a large roll-in shower, a pedestal washbowl and a center floor drain. One clothes closet has a lowered shirt pole and lower shelves. Electrical switches are three-way inside and outside, with receptacles about three feet up from the floor. Kitchen base cabinets have full access drawers with storage for china, cups, pans, etc., and the stove has controls on the front. A dining countertop/bar is positioned at wheelchair height with a small TV on an adjustable wall bracket. The door of the airtight wood-burning stove is at a convenient height.

East Dummerston, Vermont

Juliet Cuming and David Shaw didn't just build a home; they literally turned it into a production. With a background in filmmaking, the husband/wife team felt that knowledge about sustainable building technologies was critically needed, so they decided to shoot a documentary chronicling the creation of their own natural house. Along the way they founded a nonprofit organization to promote the concept called Earth Sweet Home.

Their passion resulted from their own educational process. Like many chemically sensitive people, it took years for Juliet to make the connection between her health problems and the toxic materials she encountered in urban daily life. As she and David explored their options for living in a chemical-free environment, they decided to start from scratch in southern Vermont and to encourage and empower others by example. Their goal was to demonstrate that sustainable building strategies require no sacrifice in comfort and aesthetics.

They set high standards for themselves and achieved them with few compromises. Sustainable principles suggest using local or on-site nontoxic low-embodied-energy materials, hiring local craftspeople to work on the project, choosing products that are durable and long-lasting, eliminating indoor pollution with nontoxic cleaning and decorating products, and incorporating renewable energy sources for an independent home. The challenge was set.

They decided on a compact, boxy 2 1/2-story design that would be easy to heat in the cold Vermont winters, and considered feng shui and baubiology (healthy building) principles throughout. A high-mass masonry heater, perhaps the most efficient of wood-burning stoves, was chosen as the heating system. It has worked so well that Juliet and David never bothered to hook up their backup baseboard heating system.

Eschewing energy-intensive cement, David worked alongside a local craftsman to create a dry-stacked stone foundation, gathering materials from old rock walls on the property. The timber frame is fabricated from locally milled hemlock, an underutilized forest resource, and their straw bales came from just across the border in Massachusetts. They plastered the exterior with lime/cement stucco and used on-site earth for the interior base coats. For the final finish, Juliet chose a lime wash for its natural antibacterial qualities. In the attic is a thick layer of cellulose insulation made from recycled newspaper treated with a fire retardant. A generous three-foot overhang of the long-lasting metal roof sheds snow and rain away from the bale walls.

The home is flooded with natural light through south, east and west windows, while north windows were kept small by design. They chose to install super-efficient windows made regionally, called Ultra-Glass, which incorporate two low-e films to achieve a middle-of-the-glass R-value of 9. The attic, which they have developed as office space, has operable skylights and tubular skylights for light, heat and venting.

Solar collectors supply most of their hot water, which is boosted if necessary by an on-demand water heater. And their electrical energy is supplied by a 1-kilowatt photovoltaic system combined with a 1.5-kilowatt wind turbine, with the occasional use of a propane

This handsome two-story, passive-solar home was built almost entirely with local materials and by local craftsmen.

The efficient wood-burning masonry heater is located at the center of the activity space, where cooking, dining, and home-schooling happen.

South-facing windows create a bright, comfortable living room and library.

Upper Level

S

Ground Level

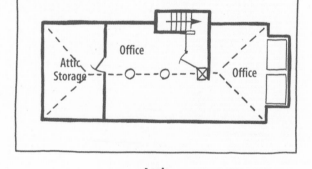

Attic

To conserve heat, the north-facing front enters into a separate mudroom, as an air lock, and the second-floor windows were kept small.

back-up generator. While conscious of their power consumption, this household has it all: a washer, dishwasher, color TV, VCR, stereo system, two computers, printer, fax and scanner. Furnishings and draperies are also fashioned with natural materials, including cotton and hemp fabrics. They are pleased with their choices but admit "there's not one way to design or build; it's just developing an awareness."

Although the documentary is on the back burner for now, Juliet and David's house is serving its purpose. They open it for organized tours of solar homes in the area, and have inspired dozens of rural Vermont residents to build their own natural homes. Most importantly, Juliet's health has improved significantly. And they are raising their son, Hunter, in a sunlit, natural, earth sweet home.

Square footage: 2,500 interior
4 bedrooms, 2 baths + home office, 2 ½ stories, post-and-beam
Architect: Owner-designed and built
Timber frame: Dan MacArthur
Solar electrician: Richard Gottlieb,
    Sunnyside Solar
Wind system: Ed Knott, Bannertown
    Power & Light
Cost per square foot: $75, plus energy
    systems (about $30,000)

A round strawbale shed with a "living roof" stores the PV batteries and other necessities.

A long driveway leads to the Howells' private residence, Trinity House.

Crestone, Colorado

Sanctuary House, a spiritual retreat center at the foot of the Sangre de Cristo Mountains near Crestone, Colorado, is a religious and educational nonprofit founded by Barbara and William Howell. Through its very presence, it seeks to educate people about sustainability and provide a model of living more simply.

The complex of buildings provides several beautifully finished examples of strawbale construction, from the circular retreat center to a caretaker's residence to the most recently completed structure—an elegant home for Barbara and William, called Trinity House.

The Howells have consistently chosen straw bales for their buildings for several reasons. Says William, "Perhaps first is their beauty. Strawbale architecture offers a feeling of strength in its mass, yet a feminine sense in its curves and undulations—a quality unmatchable in traditional frame houses. Second, the cost is about the same as a conventional frame house, yet look at what you get! Third, the interior space, compared to other building methods, is far cooler in the summer and warmer in the winter by virtue of the fine insulation values. And, finally, the material itself is so clean, and the bales so versatile in their plasticity."

The Howells sheltered their home against a small hill and built up two stories to take advantage of the views. Sun streams into the living/dining areas through south-facing windows, while windows on the north were intentionally kept small.

A glassed entry room creates an air-lock space and a convenient place to remove shoes before stepping into a spacious and serene living/dining/kitchen area. An adjacent sunroom has been adapted to guest use, and a small library/office completes the first floor. Above are two separate bedrooms joined by a private deck with a hot tub open to the heavens.

Despite lenient building codes, the architect chose a post-and-beam framework for Trinity House due to its two-story height and the number of windows, which require structural rigidity. Straw bales infill the walls (except against the hill), which are protected by a metal roof insulated with six inches of rigid foam. Commercial stucco finishes were applied inside and out.

The centerpiece of the Sanctuary House complex is a circular courtyard surrounded by four guest rooms with a shared kitchen, and four shrine/meditation rooms representing the major religious traditions: Jewish/Christian, Buddhist/Zen, Hindu/Vedic, and Sufi/Muslim. The complex is crafted from locally harvested logs and colored clays for the plasters and floors, and, of course, straw bales.

Sanctuary House includes a private home, a caretaker's house, plus a circular courtyard complex with four meditation rooms and three guest bedrooms surrounding a labyrinth.

A majestic juniper tree harvested from the site now welcomes visitors as they step inside Trinity House. It is also incorporated into the structure.

The courtyard walls shelter a replication of the eleven-tiered circular labyrinth of Chartres, known as the *dromenon*. The labyrinth, directed toward Crestone Peak, was poured in forms and troweled with an antique gold finish. Despite the solemnity of this space, a warm sense of welcome and hospitality envelops those who enter. The labyrinth offers a powerful opportunity for walking meditation. It symbolizes the hopeful spiritual journey that every soul is making: There are no false turns (as in a maze), and its form implies that by putting one foot in front of the other, one will arrive at the

Overnight guest rooms are booked for individual and group retreats.

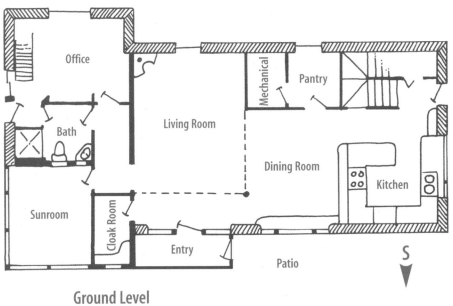

Office

Mechanical

Pantry

Living Room

Bath

Dining Room

Kitchen

Sunroom

Cloak Room

Entry

Patio

S

Ground Level

This private corner offers a peaceful place to sit. Sanctuary guests share a common kitchen and library.

goal of life. The Howells are part of a modern movement to reintroduce labyrinths, an ancient form of "sacred geometry," into our consciousness, on the grounds of hospitals, nursing homes, community centers, schools, etc., as a tool for nondogmatic spiritual growth.

The Howells delight in hosting special events and celebrations that engender the feeling of an extended community. "The final product is quite exquisite—indeed, better than the drawings look," says William. "I wanted a feeling of strength, yet simplicity. The strawbale approach was the perfect medium."

Square footage: 2,010 interior, 2,260 exterior
2 bedrooms + library and sunroom, 2 baths, 2 stories, post-and-beam
Architect: Touson Saryon, Integral Design Studio
Builder: Paul Koppana, Sky Hawk Construction
Feng shui consultant: Robin Cheri
Earthen floors: Jonathan Bruce
Approximate cost per square foot: $100

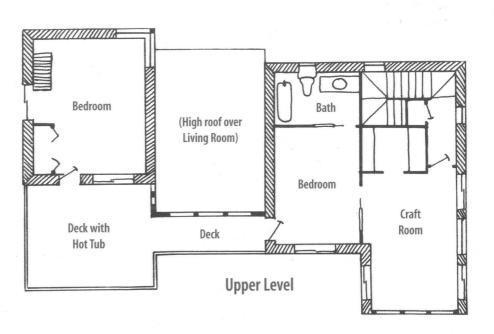

Bedroom

(High roof over Living Room)

Bath

Bedroom

Craft Room

Deck with Hot Tub

Deck

Upper Level

Family Havens

For a family, home should be a haven and much more. A healthy environment—which means nontoxic building materials and the ability to flood the home with fresh air and sunlight—can dramatically improve family life. Even non-organic straw bales are benign to build with, and since bale finishes are typically plaster, this nearly eliminates the need for interior paints and the variety of toxic ingredients they often contain. Clay plaster is considered a healthy choice and lime has antibacterial properties, so some select it as a final wash for kitchen and bathrooms.

A good family design is functional and easy to clean. Stained-concrete floors are a common choice for their beauty, durability and cost. Mudrooms are useful as catchalls for soiled clothes and shoes. In a cold climate, well-sealed self-closing doors will eliminate a major source of heat loss.

Easy access to safe outdoor space is also a necessity. An increasingly popular concept for families is cohousing, which combines the privacy of single-family homes with the community of an old-fashioned neighborhood.

A well-designed floor plan encourages interactive family togetherness while allowing for individual privacy. A home can even inspire learning and creativity, especially in the building process. During the straw bale wall raising, children often join in the fun as part of the building team. They can help stack bales, stuff the cracks, sweep up or just play around in a pile of soft, squishy straw. Plastering with earth is another kid-friendly process—imagine a child *not* wanting to play in the mud. Building naturally can be a bonding experience for a family, and inevitably the long-term impact is empowering.

Orangeville, Ontario, Canada

A chance meeting with architect Linda Chapman introduced David and Anne-Marie Warburton to the concept of straw bale construction, and it seemed to them like a sensible idea. So when they found a wooded parcel of land near Orangeville, Ontario, they hired Linda to realize their vision of an Adirondack-style strawbale home.

A self-employed couple, David and Anne-Marie were initially challenged to finance their dream house. But persistence paid off, and they finally found a loan officer who was actually excited about their plans. Design limitations included positioning the structure away from the floodplain of an adjacent river and their desire to cut as few trees as possible. After creating a south-facing clearing for their building site, the Warburtons ultimately used all the trees cut down in the construction of their home.

David and Anne-Marie decided on a two-story floor plan for economy of building and heating. Bedrooms for this family of four are all on the second floor, with one shared bath. A large dormer combined with an oversized landing makes a functional family room centrally located between bedrooms. Downstairs, a Temp-Cast masonry heater is the centerpiece between kitchen/dining and living rooms, with hers and his offices adjacent. A large mudroom entryway is a necessity for living in the country, as children and dogs flow constantly in and out, donning and discarding hats, coats, boots and bones.

The Warburtons employed an engineer for the structural design and to certify the sizes of round and rough-cut lumber used. They were also required to install an alternative septic system because of their proximity to the river. Per climate requirements, the concrete foundation is four feet deep and is topped by an insulated slab. The heating system includes the central masonry heater, augmented by radiant floor heat. While most of the double-glazed argon-filled windows face south, passive solar gain is limited by cloudy winter weather—though the glass does allow in much-needed natural light.

Anne-Marie acted as the general contractor, coordinating the variety of building subcontractors, which was a mostly positive learning experience. She remembers the first day of the wall raising as a festive event: the kids were excited, there were fifty people on hand (only a third of whom she knew), and there was Linda, directing the whole affair on crutches. Though they stacked nearly nine hundred bales that day, to the Warburtons it felt less like work than a celebration.

Salvaged pine boards from a Planters Peanuts factory became their wood floors, local larch trees were utilized for structure, excellent bales bought from a local farmer made up the walls, and the attic was insulated with blown-in cellulose. An antique sink and fixtures make their kitchen seem like grandma's.

A dormer window space creates a comfortable nook on the second-floor landing, which functions as a family entertainment space, and doubles as a guest bedroom.

This Adirondack-style home with its enchanting landscape is commuting distance from the urban center of Toronto.

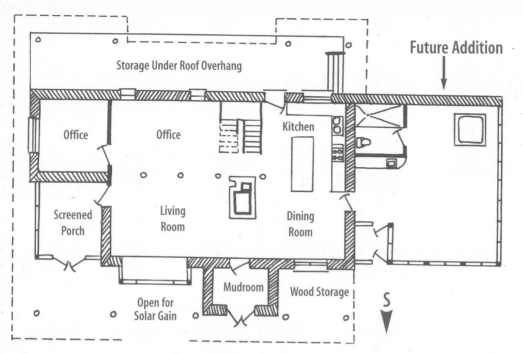

Storage Under Roof Overhang

Future Addition

Office

Office

Kitchen

Screened Porch

Living Room

Dining Room

Open for Solar Gain

Mudroom

Wood Storage

S

Upper Level

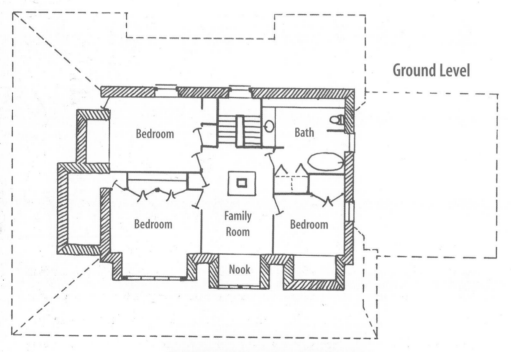

Ground Level

Bedroom

Bath

Bedroom

Family Room

Bedroom

Nook

The relaxed living room features an oversized window seat for lounging.

Wood framing around the window is evidence of the meticulous craftsmanship throughout this house.

Bales are plastered with a three-coat lime/cement stucco, with iron oxide pigments for color. Wood twigs with bark intact were used for exterior trim, in true Adirondack style. Finally, David, a landscape designer, created a specimen garden in the front yard and nursery plots to the side. It is a natural setting for the children to play within and a delight for visitors to experience.

The stucco process was the most stressful, say the Warburtons, for a number of reasons. Inevitably, the schedule slipped, and the stucco job planned in September happened in December, with the threat of severe freezing. The inexperienced stucco crew underbid the job and then scrimped on the details, neglecting to seal the joints between the bale and the exposed timber frame. This led to air infiltration and a chilly first winter. They had this repaired before the *next* winter.

Still, the Warburtons remain passionate about building with bales, and open their home regularly for educational tours. They advise getting the floor plan right because "you have to live with that forever." And they offer this encouragement: "Follow your dreams. It really is that good."

Square footage: 2,100 interior, 2,572 exterior
3 bedrooms, 2 baths, + office, 2 stories, post-and-beam
Architect: Linda Chapman
Carpentry: Colin Cherry, Michael Ash
Approximate cost per square foot: $95 (Canadian)

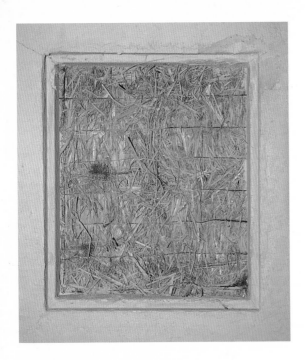

Mill Valley, California

In the densely settled suburb of Mill Valley, California, Greg and Marian Breeze wanted to make a statement by building an ecological home in connection with its natural surroundings as a place to raise their family. Though fortunate to have a plot adjacent to Greg's parents' house, they saved for years to build a home of their own in the high-dollar real estate market of northern California. With architects David Arkin and Annie Tilt, they designed a functional and child-friendly space in a smaller-than-average size.

In this "no shoes" household, the entry offers a convenient spot to sit and change to slippers. One enters into a light-filled great room that combines living, dining and kitchen space for this family of five that likes to be with each other. The ceiling height rises from eight feet to sixteen feet in the cupola/clerestory, which creates a dramatic space and illuminates activities with natural light that changes throughout the day. These high windows also provide solar heat and allow ventilation.

The long wall that separates living space from bedrooms is also a structural solution for sheer stability during seismic events. It does triple duty as a wall of storage. Other space-saving features include built-in alcove beds and sliding pocket doors. There's even a sliding door between the girls' bedrooms that closes for privacy and opens to create a large play space they can share.

The open floor plan is easy to
clean, and the children have
lots of space to play in sight of
an adult.

Marian encourages her children to be comfortable indoors and out. Doors open on
three sides of the home to a large yard with a playhouse and pet goats. When the kids get
dirty, cleanup is a "breeze"—a door opens directly from outside into the roomy master-
bath shower, equipped with two showerheads. Floors are a blue-green scored concrete that
takes abuse and is easy to clean.

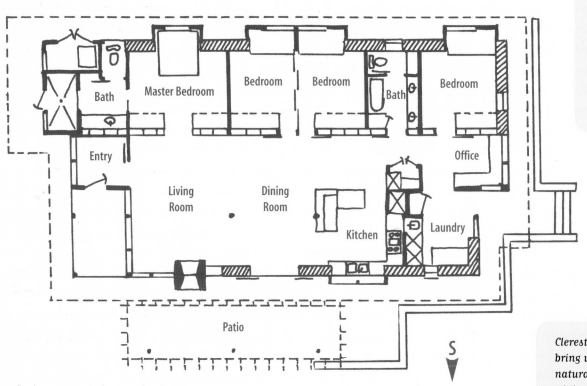

The round interior post is a eucalyptus tree harvested from the site. The center wall is engineered to provide sheer strength and does triple duty as a storage wall.

Clerestory windows bring volumes of natural light inside, while wide porches extend the living area into the outdoors in this coastal California climate.

Bath

Master Bedroom

Bedroom

Bedroom

Bath

Bedroom

Entry

Office

Living Room

Dining Room

Kitchen

Laundry

Patio

S

The Breezes chose to use sustainably harvested lumber throughout, much of it milled on-site. Eucalyptus trees cut down on the spot were utilized as shapely interior posts. Other "green" materials include salvaged doors, "Hardi-plank" for exterior siding, and a recycled-glass terrazzo countertop in the master bath—an ecological work of art. Rye-grass panels lend a clean yet textural finish to non-strawbale walls and ceilings. The kitchen features Ikea cabinets, built-in recycling bins accessible from the outside, and a compost collector right in the cutting block. The bale walls are finished with sprayed-on, soil-cement plaster—smooth on the inside, but left with a rough texture on the exterior—reminiscent of a Tuscan farmhouse.

The Breeze home also embraces the twenty-first century, evidenced by its metal roof, industrial-style chimneys and sleek lines. A computer industry professional, Greg had wiring integrated throughout to accommodate emerging "smart house" technology. Building during the height of the Silicon Valley boom caused costs to skyrocket, due primarily to high labor costs and custom features, not materials. But because of their prime location, their real estate investment should be secure.

And their personal investment is incalculable. Says Greg, "One of the joys of this project was being involved in the actual building, the hefting of bales." Wherever possible, Marian encouraged the children to participate, as in decorating tiles to be installed in their bathroom. Now settled into their live-lightly lifestyle, the Breeze family is thriving.

Square footage: 1,664 interior, 1,860 exterior
4 bedrooms, 2 baths, 1 story, post-and-beam
Architect: Arkin Tilt Architects, Annie Tilt and David Arkin, AIA, ADPSR
Builder : Neal McDonald, McDonald Builders
Approximate cost per square foot: Not available

Eden Mills, Ontario, Canada

Surrounded by farmland and within commuting distance of Toronto, historic Eden Mills is where Glenn and Libby Little chose to create their personal Eden. They wanted to raise their two young sons in a healthy home and a family-oriented community. So far, so good!

The Littles chose strawbale for its energy efficiency and to utilize a regional "waste material." Referred to local cutting-edge architect Charles Simon, Libby clipped some home styles from the newspaper to show their preferences and discovered that Simon had designed them! With drawings stamped by an architect and a building inspector familiar with bale construction, the permit process went through without a hitch.

They decided on a two-story rectilinear shape for its clean lines and cost efficiency. The mudroom entry is the exception, adding visual interest and providing a great place to ditch muddy boots and dirty toys. It's also essential for energy efficiency, as it provides an air lock to keep cold air from sweeping through the house when the front door is opened. A handsome Temp-Cast masonry heater faced with brick serves as a divider between living and dining rooms, and as their primary heat source. Since building in cold country requires a deep foundation anyway, the Littles chose to incorporate nine-foot ceilings in the basement, to make it really livable. In retrospect, they would have added an exterior entrance to give the basement more versatility as a potential rental unit.

Passive solar orientation insures that light and heat flood the sleek contemporary living and dining and rooms, and upstairs bedrooms. Eschewing air-conditioning, they open windows at night as a cooling strategy. Lower windows on the north draw in the cool night breeze, replacing warm indoor air, which is vented out through a skylight above the staircase. Libby loves having fresh air flow through the house, as it brings back childhood memories of the fragrant summer breeze. French doors on the south let them open up the front of the house, giving her the feeling of an open-air cafe within the comfort of her dining room.

Glenn acted as the general contractor, hiring subcontractors for almost everything and keeping on top of all the details. He chose batts of mineral wool for ceiling insulation, and a forced-air backup heating system. During the five months of construction, Glenn was challenged to keep the straw dry during inclement weather. "Pick a dry summer," he jokes. He also recommends digging the foundation as early as possible, and "if you can't start early, put it off a year." On the whole, the Littles are really happy with their home and about meeting a network of interesting people during the building process. Glenn remarks, "I'm glad I did it, and I'm glad I can check it off my life list of things to do."

Square footage: 2,300 interior
3 bedrooms, 2 ½ baths, 2-story +1,300 basement, post-and-beam
Architect: Charles Simon
Builder: Owner-built, with subcontractors
Approximate cost per square foot: $100 (Canadian)

Oriented to the south for maximum passive solar gain, the two-story rectangle is an economical shape to build.

A handsome masonry stove provides heat and visual separation between the contemporary living room and dining area—where it conveniently contains a built-in pizza oven.

The formal dining room features a large fixed window for view and seating, while the kitchen windows open for ventilation.

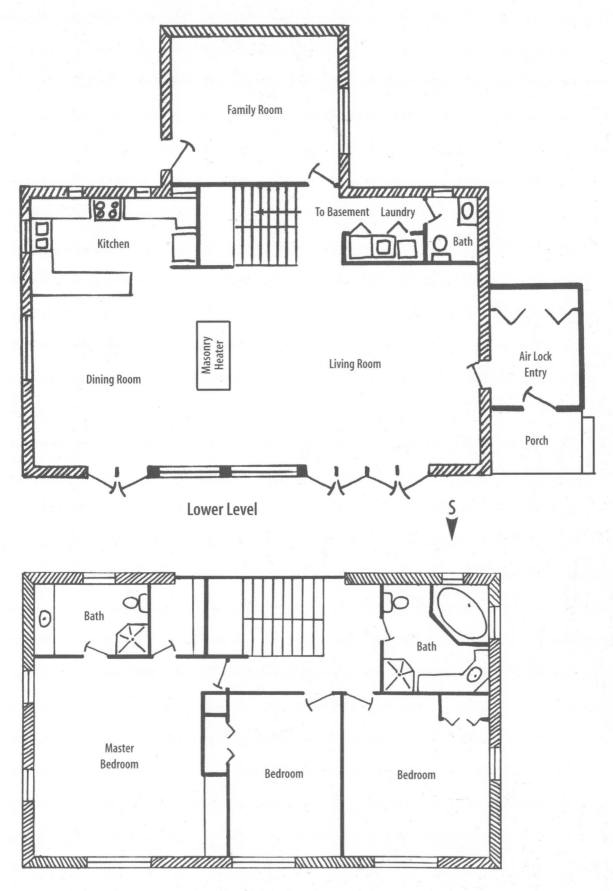

Family Room

Kitchen

To Basement   Laundry

Bath

Masonry Heater

Living Room

Dining Room

Air Lock Entry

Porch

Lower Level

S

Bath

Bath

Master Bedroom

Bedroom

Bedroom

Upper Level

Centreville, Ontario, Canada

Rising from the fields of wheat from whence it began, the strawbale home of organic farmer and retired town councilman John Wise and his wife, Anita Jansman, has become a new landmark in Stone Mills Township, Ontario. John had always been fascinated by "widow's walk" observation platforms in seacoast communities, so when it came time to design their family home, he decided to incorporate this little bit of "luxury." Up in his tower, John is lord of all he surveys—a hundred-acre organic farm growing berries, vegetables, grain, chickens and ten beef cows.

Actually very down-to-earth people, John and Anita were attracted to strawbale as an environmentally sensible alternative to conventional stud-frame construction. They discussed their preferences with Toronto architect Janet Stewart, including cathedral ceilings, a loft bedroom, a screened-in porch, a built-in pantry, and the observation tower. Her compact design incorporated all this, plus a sewing room for Anita, an office for John and two bedrooms in the basement for their sons.

In cold climates, foundation requirements mean digging down below the frost line, naturally creating a basement level. This below-ground space is ideal for the boys, who spend plenty of time outside on the farm, then retreat to their basement suite to watch TV or play computer games. On the ground floor, the kitchen/dining space opens into a living room with cathedral ceiling and is illuminated by a wall of south-facing glass. Above the kitchen, the master bedroom is open to the living room below. A ladder from John's office leads up to his observation tower. Anita and John appreciate their floor plan: "Janet made a small space feel like a big space."

Getting a permit and insurance was fairly routine. The local code official had experience with strawbale, plus their plans had an engineer's stamp on them. And their insurance agent was a reasonable person. Overall, the process was very harmonious.

The organic wheat straw was baled on-site, including custom bales per calculations. The tall structure required using a bale elevator to place the bales in the walls.

The tower was built on the ground and hoisted into place with a crane. John remembers, "It was tremendous fun having the bale-raising crew around. They understood my jokes!"

Unfortunately, the initial drawing had a mistake in the width of the stairs, which translated into the trusses being off. This didn't compromise the structure but required time-consuming adjustment. Also, a wet year prevented an early harvest of the straw, which, combined with the usual delays, had them finishing the lime/cement stuccoing in November, in the cold. The family moved in on December 1, with a bit of interior finish work still to complete.

The ground floor is textured, stamped concrete with radiant floor heat and a woodstove for backup. Anita found there's a heating advantage with an open floor plan, as heat can rise and circulate freely. This is not an advantage when it comes to noise, however. "You'd better all be going to bed at the same time," she warns. The stairwell transfers sound, too, which resonates up through the wood framework from the boys' game room. The Wises plan to add a door at the bottom of the stairs for more sound isolation. John believes they are saving money on utilities but admits that energy efficiency is compromised by the large space of windows and their windy site.

Overall, they are more than satisfied. John advises, "Do your homework and talk to as many people as you can who have experience. Then give yourself as much lead time as possible."

Square footage: 2,200 interior
3 bedrooms, 2 baths, 3 stories with tower, post-and-beam
Architect: Janet Stewart
Builder: Chris Magwood, Peter Mack, and Tina Therrien,
    Camel's Back Construction
Approximate cost per square foot: $100 (Canadian)

This strawbale tower has become a local landmark in an agricultural region of Ontario.

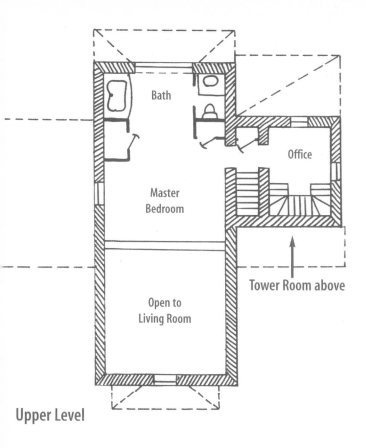

Upper Level

Bath

Office

Master
Bedroom

Tower Room above

Open to
Living Room

The window from the master bedroom offers a sweeping view of the Wise family's organic farm.

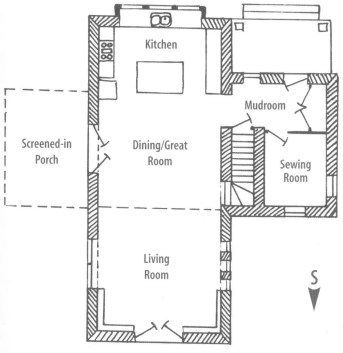

Kitchen

Screened-in
Porch

Dining/Great
Room

Mudroom

Sewing
Room

Living
Room

S

Ground Level

Adjacent to the kitchen and a screened-in porch, the great room is the place where the family gathers.

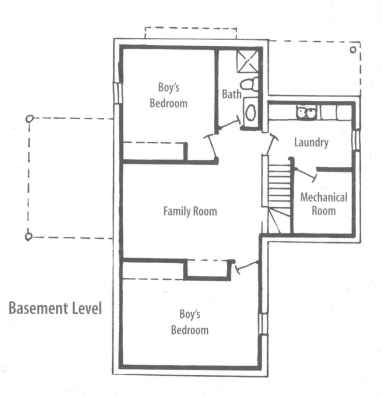

Boy's
Bedroom

Bath

Laundry

Family Room

Mechanical
Room

Boy's
Bedroom

Basement Level

Whidbey Island, Washington

While property hunting for friends on Whidbey Island, Washington, Scott and Marie Burnett saw the potential of a seven-acre, partially-wooded plot and made an offer on it, imagining how they could raise their children in this restful rural setting.

Though they were attracted to the aesthetics of strawbale, straw seemed counterintuitive for the rainy climate of the Pacific Northwest, so they looked at a lot of other building options. "We systematically tried to establish reasons why we shouldn't build with straw and couldn't defeat the proposition," as Scott puts it.

The Burnetts set about creating their own design, but discovered it was difficult to communicate their ideas to each other and find agreement. After Scott attended a strawbale workshop with architect Chris Stafford, they hired him to help. As Scott explains, "Chris was the cheapest marriage therapy that I can imagine. He helped us take complex ideas and explain them to each other."

Their final design includes cathedral ceilings that allow room for a variety of lofts and also exude the drama of an intimate space emerging into an expansive one. Their four children have individual small bedrooms, each with a window

Floor-to-ceiling bookshelves are a creative solution to maximizing storage space.

seat and a tiny loft space. Above the master bedroom, Scott has an office loft with a view. Off the dining/great room is a music/playroom separated by sound-dampening strawbale interior walls—essential when the Irish fiddle and bagpipes are getting warmed up. Says Scott, "We all sleep on one side and eat and have activities on the other. And it allows for people to sleep while people are active on the other side of the house."

They sited the house in a clearing on a small hill, so rain will naturally drain away from the foundation. A sun-catching entry porch and south-facing windows make the most of this climate's scarce sunshine. The Burnetts chose to build a load-bearing bale structure, confident in their architect and the engineering calculations.

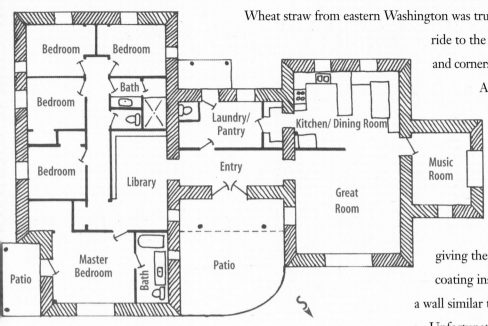

Wheat straw from eastern Washington was trucked in, taking the twenty-minute ferry ride to the island. Bales were pinned with bamboo, and corners were tied together with packing banding.

A continuous wooden bond beam, or top plate, connects the bale walls and structure at the top of the tall bale walls. The top plate is strapped to the foundation, and the roof is attached to it. The weight of this assembly compresses the bale walls, giving them more solidity. A cement/lime stucco coating inside and out also adds stability, creating a wall similar to a stress-skin panel.

Unfortunately, the day after the wall raising, an unexpected storm caught the builders by surprise and the walls got wet. Rain followed the path of the bamboo pins down into the center of the bales, and serious water damage ensued. While work continued on the building, large fans were brought in to aid the drying process. Moisture monitoring indicated where the walls were too wet, and eventually the Burnetts dug out areas of decomposing straw and replaced them with fresh. Finally, the moisture probes indicated the walls were sufficiently dry and it was safe to stucco them. Years later, there is no hint of mold or its telltale odor. But the Burnetts advise: Always tarp your exposed bales to avoid this unnecessary headache.

Square footage: 2,385 interior, including 435 loft space, 2,600 exterior
5 bedrooms + music room, 2 ½ baths, 1 ½ stories, load-bearing
Architect: Chris Stafford
Builders: Carl Magnusson, David Mergens and Ron Lewis
Stucco: Joe Sager
Approximate cost per square foot: $110

FAR LEFT: In the dense woods and cloudy climate of the Pacific Northwest, the gray color of concrete stucco blends in. The Burnetts are still deciding on a final color.

LEFT: Lofts make use of the vertical space in a home with high ceilings.

RIGHT: A formal but friendly entry hallway connects the living/dining space and the bedroom wing.

Applegate Valley, Oregon

The west wing is connected to the common space with a glassed-in corridor.

Although the nuclear family has become the norm in America, it wasn't so many decades ago that extended families lived together for economic and social reasons. In the Applegate Valley of southern Oregon, two sisters, Maud and Cinda Macrory, and their husbands and children are revisiting this old-fashioned living arrangement with an interesting twist. They created a home combining the best of both worlds: individual space to have necessary privacy and a common space to enjoy the benefits of community living.

Maud and Cinda combined their resources to buy and build a unique strawbale home on a 180-acre parcel. The central community house with its common kitchen is the meeting place, library, kids' playroom and living/dining room. Attached wings serve as the private living space for each family, including offices, bedrooms and bathrooms. Only one set of utilities had to be installed, plus they share appliances—refrigerator, freezer, stove, etc.—as well as the work of cooking, cleaning and maintenance.

Architect John Duffie came up with stylish corridors to connect the spaces. One family travels a glass hallway to their private wing and the other connects via a second-floor-view walkway. A sunroom addition and clerestory windows invite solar gain in the winter, while tall ceilings and high vent windows allow the rising heat to escape in the summer. Inside temperatures also benefit from the shade provided by wide overhangs and two large walnut trees on the west.

A durable metal roof insulated with two sheets of rigid foam caps the post-and-beam structure. Easy-care colored-concrete floors were poured for the ground-level rooms, with wood floors on the other levels. They utilized decorative and functional local stone, natural slate in the bathrooms and cement/lime stucco inside and out, virtually eliminating the need for paint in the house.

Energy-saving technologies were incorporated into the design, including rooftop solar collectors that preheat water, a cistern to collect rainwater for irrigation, double-paned windows, compact fluorescent light bulbs and low-water-use appliances. Photovoltaic panels provide 60 percent of their electrical energy without need for batteries, as they benefit from a grid intertie. The families are enthusiastic about their low utility bills but wish they had been able to install a gray-water system as well.

During the fifteen months of construction on this large, complex building, the owners had difficulties coordinating the timing of all the subcontractors. Concerned about the interior plaster drying before the onset of cold weather, they initiated the plastering before the floors, doors and windows were complete. According to Cinda's husband, Dicken Weatherby, "In our experience, plastering of the inside and out does not require any particular expertise in working with straw. The general plasterers were very efficient and fast."

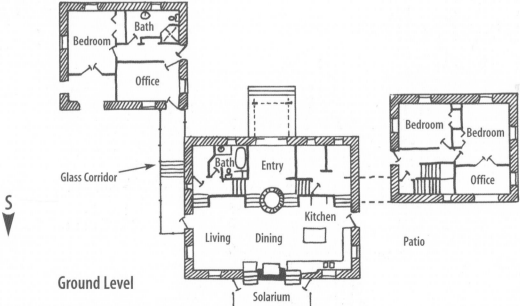

Ground Level

"If you are doing a post-and-beam structure, get the most experienced and best contractor available," Dicken suggests, "regardless of their experience with strawbale. You can always hire a strawbale consultant to handle that phase of construction." While the families feel that the community house could have been smaller with a more efficient use of space, the "wing" structures work great for them. "The benefits of this situation are tremendous savings in construction costs, and supportive social interaction."

Square footage: 3,530 interior, 4,470 exterior
4 bedrooms, 3 baths 2 stories, post-and-beam
Architect: John David Duffie
Permaculture consultant: Tom Ward
Approximate cost per square foot: $105

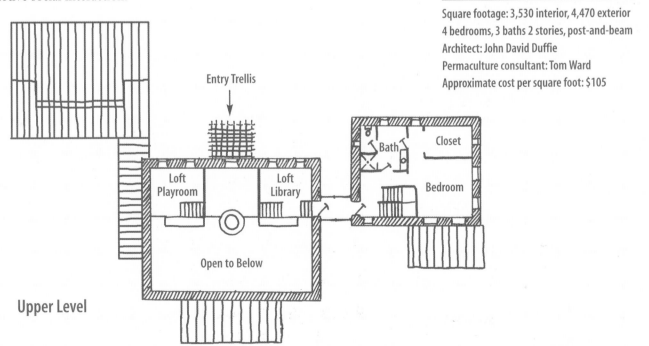

Entry Trellis

Loft Playroom

Loft Library

Bath

Closet

Bedroom

Open to Below

Upper Level

Whidbey Island, Washington
(Maxwelton Creek Cohousing)

On rural Whidbey Island, Washington, close to the bus line,
shopping and schools, a narrow lane leads to Maxwelton
Creek Cohousing. The wooded driveway opens to a crescent-
shaped parking lot flanked by blackberry bushes, where
cohousing members park and walk to their homes. The circle
of six houses is clustered above and behind a line of trees that
screens them from the road. For fire code reasons, homes are
a minimum of fifty feet apart. The community has room for
two more, plus a "common house" planned to be built in
2003 that will house shared laundry and cooking facilities,
plus a large dining room big enough for the whole
community.

The homes, on half-acre lots, are privately owned, and all
but one are strawbale. Members met weekly for several years
as they searched for land and explored the values they wanted
to embody in their homes and community. Embracing the
ethic of low environmental impact, they agreed to limit each
home's footprint to 1,500 square feet. Other strategies
included solar orientation, maximum insulation, the use of
recycled and salvaged materials, and water conservation.

The total land they hold in common is twenty-one acres
of rolling meadow, pasture and forest. Much of the land is in
permanent conservation status. In the long term, the
community is committed to restoring salmon to Maxwelton
Creek, which runs through the property.

Burlington, Vermont (Ten Stones Community)

"It takes a village to raise a child," asserts Gillian Comstock, a mother of three and a veteran of living in communities. She has put down roots at Ten Stones Community near Burlington, Vermont, a ten-year-old community with eighteen households, including thirty adults and sixteen children. Her neighbors are mostly baby boomers, now mature couples in their forties and fifties, many having had children later in life. But also in residence are two grandmothers—one who needs care and one who is helping her single-mom daughter care for her daughter. Most have professional careers such as engineer, physician, chiropractor, therapist, etc. They need to, as it's not cheap to build a home and live in this part of Vermont, where taxes and expenses are high.

Gillian and her husband, Russell, have three teen-aged sons, one just off to college. As a young mother, Gillian was worried about being isolated in a nuclear family, and so they sought out alternatives. Having grown up in a variety of community situations and having spent the last five years at Ten Stones Community, their sons are self-reliant, which Gillian feels is partly a benefit of having other adults in their lives as role models, mentors and friends.

"Ten Stones is truly 'kid heaven,'" Gillian states, "They don't have to get in a car to go play. And the latch-key child just doesn't exist here—there's always a neighbor's home to go to." Parents feel supported by other parents and make a variety of child-care arrangements.

Cohousing is a revival of the ancient form of the cluster village, and though it has been around for decades in Denmark, in North America it is still a cultural experiment. Ten Stones looks like a neighborhood development, but members have common stewardship of their jointly owned natural resources and there is a greater intention to share their lives. Since decisions are made by consensus, cohousing requires clear communication and a basic intention to find agreement for the common good. There is a personal learning curve about how to live in such a community that includes self-knowledge and the releasing of judgment and blame.

This can be challenging for Americans raised with the ideas of privatism and personal gratification. Gillian believes this implies a powerful paradigm shift from the owning model to a deeper way of viewing our neighbors—a certain willingness to see ourselves as connected, all part of the same web of life. This requires taking care of relationships and dealing with unavoidable conflict. At Ten Stones there are regular opportunities to practice these personal skills; while attendance at biweekly business meetings is not required, this is where consensus is

Every corner inside this small home is used efficiently.

sought for decisions affecting the whole community. Members also meet at their one-acre Community Supported Agriculture (CSA) garden, where everyone pitches in to grow, harvest and share a plethora of organic produce. The CSA also involves nearby towns and other neighbors, evidence that there's not an insider/outsider mentality here. A fruit orchard and an organic compost company also help utilize the eighty stewarded acres.

Typically, cohousing communities come together at least weekly for a shared meal, which also engenders close relationships. But Ten Stones has not yet built their "common house," so there is not a space large enough for a community meal. Members do envision a "bio house" for the whole community to gather, powered by solar and wind energy systems and including a greenhouse and root cellar. In the meantime, they all get together outside for various festivals and celebrations throughout the year.

Homes are positioned in an eight-acre spiral pattern, with vehicle access around the outside and a grassy "green" between the houses. Each household has a half-acre lot on which to build, honoring covenants that include moderate environmental ethics. Of sixteen homes, five families chose to build with straw bales, including the Comstocks.

The idea to build energy-efficient strawbale homes was introduced to Ten Stones by a member returning from an "ecovillage" conference, who generated enthusiasm among several other members. So by the hot summer of 1997, five households were all building with bales at the same time. Because everyone traded information, even though each family did it their own way, the learning curve was lessened by the cooperation and excitement they shared.

While cohousing is their "neo-village," Ten Stones members are involved in local activities and town politics as well. Their professions and the CSA maintain a positive impression within the greater community, and their children attend local public and alternative schools. The commitment to cooperation and the inner work this requires pays off in deeper relationships with neighbors. But the next generation may be the true beneficiaries. Gillian watched entranced one day as a small boy, almost too young, determinedly made his first independent walk across their village green over to the home of his playmate. Of course, there was a mother at a window in both directions, watching the whole way.

A strawbale duplex faces the central playground, so parents can keep an eye on their children through the windows.

Bayfield, Colorado (Heartwood Cohousing)

As a founder and community leader of Heartwood Cohousing near Bayfield, Colorado, Werner Heiber found himself in the position of also being a general contractor. Two members dropped out late in the planning stages, even though the ground had already been broken on one of the cornerstone lots of the clustered community. Werner undertook the commitment of completing the small duplex, designed for families with small children, with the confidence that "if you build it they will come."

This idealism is evident in the quality of construction. A two-story post-and-beam structure (required by code) was infilled with straw bales on both levels, topped by a pro-panel metal roof, with R-50 cellulose in the ceilings. Radiant heat warms concrete floors covered with attractive Saltillo tile. Windows are wood-framed and "low-e." Ceilings are painted with a nontoxic, low VOC paint, and both sides of the bale walls feature natural earth plaster; a dazzling aliz finishes the inside. On three sides, pant roofs over the first floor protect the earth plasters from driving rain. On the south, an arbor extension provides shade and creates a useful outdoor space. Throughout, the materials chosen are sustainable, long-lasting and low-maintenance.

The lot and house size was predetermined by the cohousing plan agreed upon by members. The two floor plans are mirror images of each other, with front doors offset for more privacy. Each unit's compact design features kitchen, dining and living space downstairs, with three bedrooms surrounding a family room upstairs. The duplex took about fourteen months to build with a small skilled crew.

Kathy Derry on Cohousing:

As we thought about moving, we asked ourselves, "What really is important to us in our living environment?" Two things immediately surfaced: that we wanted to know and be really involved with our neighbors, and that a large house isn't necessarily a better house. We surfed the 'Net and discovered the concept of cohousing. We visited one in North Carolina as well as in Colorado. The friendliness, engagement, joy and commitment of the people in Heartwood Cohousing really impressed us. During a second visit to the community a few months later, we made the decision to buy the strawbale. We brought only the things that we wanted for a new, simpler life and are as excited now about Heartwood and our neighbors as we were on our first visit. Our home is efficient as well as beautiful.

We have been very impressed with the community's willingness to share what they have. During the fires that were nearby last summer, their way of coping was to open their homes to the people who had been evacuated and support the firefighters with necessities and respite. We've lived places where we didn't feel we knew anyone well enough to ask for favors. This is a community of outreach and sharing and people living their values, while respecting our differences.

Werner is rightfully proud of the end product—its energy-efficiency and beautiful thick walls, rounded corners and meticulous finishing. This, plus the hand plastering, extra insulation, and quality materials all came at a price, which pays back in utilities savings and long-term satisfaction as one lives in the space. Werner's greatest challenges were cost overruns and trying to use the strapping system recommended by an engineer. It took some time, but he finally found the right occupants for this duplex with small, efficient floor plans.

The purchasers of duplex number one, Kathy and Brian Derry, were challenged to pare down their possessions to fit in the space, but after the job was done, they found their home "very livable. The crawl space underneath is an excellent storage space. We plan to put pocket doors in both the smaller bedrooms." Recently retired, they were attracted to the Colorado climate and this cohousing community in particular, for its vitality and openness.

Now leasing duplex number two, Terry and Steve Elfink and their two small children "love the floor plan, especially the large upstairs family room and small bedrooms. It's where we spend most of our time together." With their home office in clear sight of the playground, and other small children a hop, skip and jump away, Terry doesn't feel isolated when Steve has to travel on business. She raves, "This house has a very peaceful feeling to it. The walls and windows are beautiful on their own and don't need much decoration."

Square footage (each unit): 1,320 interior, 1,600 exterior
3 bedrooms, 2 baths, 2 stories, post-and-beam
Architect: Wayne Bingham
Builders/craftsmen: Kelly Ray Mathews, Tim White, Dennis Caufield
Approximate cost per square foot: $112

Passive solar orientation combined with the thermal mass of the living room floor helps to heat the entire house.

120

These south-facing front windows also offer a view of activities along the pedestrian street that connects all the homes in Heartwood Cohousing.

Bayfield, Colorado (Heartwood Cohousing)

Katie and Mark Waller were also attracted to the cohousing concept as a safe, nurturing environment for their children. Additionally, they resonated with Heartwood's principles of sustainability and living lightly on the land. Says Katie, "This fits with our values, and it's exciting to work together and provide an example for others to see." In building their home, this is exactly what they did.

They chose the aesthetics of a handcrafted oak timber-frame structure utilizing straw bales as infill on the north and west sides and a straw-clay infill for the south and east wall. A beautiful adobe floor takes advantage of the abundant solar gain in this southern Colorado climate. Clay plasters inside and out, finished with sparkly colored glazes, create luscious expanses of wall with all-natural materials.

The Wallers considered feng shui principles in designing their floor plan, which was a collaborative process between them, timber framer Alan Bernholz and designer/builder Kari Bremer. A private first-floor office for Katie is off the front entry but near the kitchen/living/dining area. On the second floor are three bedrooms, a bath and a multipurpose mezzanine space overlooking the downstairs. A ladder leads to an attic loft, which the boys have claimed as a personal play space. The Wallers switch the dining and living spaces seasonally: in the summer they lounge near the sunny window wall with the high ceiling, and in winter Katie prefers a cozier living space near the fireplace, and to soak up the sun at mealtimes.

"The house functions incredibly well and keeps a very comfortable climate," she says proudly. "We hardly use our heat because our soapstone stove does a great job with heating. Also, we don't need any cooling in the summer." She does admit that "although we love the

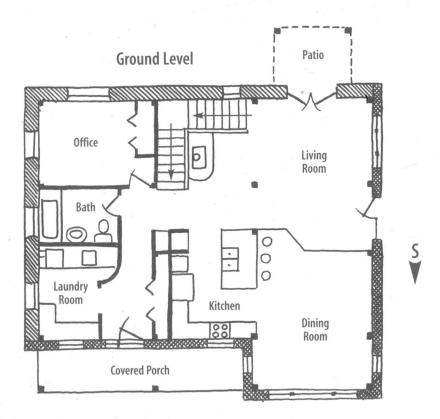

Ground Level

Patio

Office

Living Room

Bath

S

Laundry Room

Kitchen

Dining Room

Covered Porch

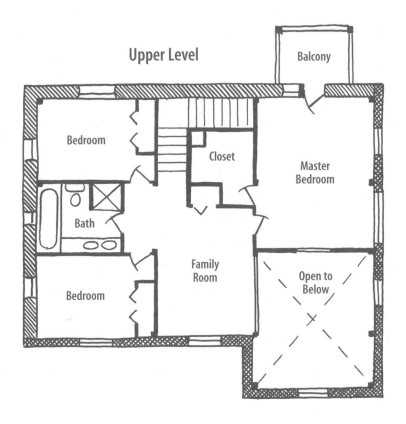

Upper Level

Balcony

Bedroom

Closet

Master Bedroom

Bath

Bedroom

Family Room

Open to Below

This sculpted adobe banister mimics stair steps to the second floor, while providing thermal mass to the fireplace area.

Katie Waller on Cohousing

It is very rich living in community, both from a supportive perspective and from a personal growth perspective. Most people that are attracted to cohousing have done a lot of work on themselves and are skilled communicators. Though it's not always easy to make decisions through consensus with forty other adults, you learn quite a bit about yourself and others. To me, it is very much like neighborhoods used to be, where people helped each other out and were good friends. We love the common meals and our cooperative home-school.

I love the concept of shared resources, i.e., 250 acres, a barn, greenhouse, workshop, hot tub and to have animals but not to have the sole responsibility for them (chickens, horses). But it takes a fair amount of work to start and run a community such as this. You have to go up against the mainstream grain and be willing to put in a lot of work.

Heartwood provides these things: wilderness without solitude, safety without being sheltered, human interaction and activity for adults and children without the chaos of running around creating social activities. And a place where our children will have many different role models and learn about cooperation and communication.

openness of the floor plan, sometimes I would like to have a quieter place to be in." And, like every family, they could use more storage space.

As it is for most families, the expense of building a custom home was their biggest concern. Katie feels that "many subs were thrown off by a different building technique. Most work was 'time and materials' rather than a bid, which I believe resulted in higher costs. Also, our 12/12 roof pitch made the SIPS panel and pro-panel installation more difficult and costly." The labor of the handcrafted natural plasters also added significantly to finishing costs. But Mark and Katie felt good about supporting their local "green builders" and their use of nontoxic materials. They love the energy efficiency and wonderful feel of their strawbale walls.

Square footage: 2,400 interior, 2,600 exterior
4 bedrooms, 2 ½ baths, 2 stories, post-and-beam
Designer/builder: Kari Bremer, Fountain of Earth Design and Construction
Builder: Steve Kawell, Fryer & Kawell Fine Homes
Timber frame: Alan Bernholtz, Wind River Timberframes
Plasters: Carole Crews, Gourmet Adobe
Approximate cost per square foot: $150

Artistic Expressions

CREATIVE PEOPLE tend to choose strawbale primarily for aesthetic reasons. For them, energy efficiency and sustainability are happy bonuses. Artists recognize that building with bales offers an opportunity to make their home their canvas.

Thick-walled straw bales can form shapely *bancos* and window seats, providing built-in comfort. They can also imitate other materials, such as stone or adobe, to evoke a European or southwestern ambiance. Bales are easily sculpted, so walls can be made to curve and undulate, and niches can be carved to display treasured objets d'art. Earthen plasters lend themselves to bas-relief, and, finished with clay slips colored with natural pigments, every wall becomes a work of art.

The homes in this chapter are highly personal expressions of each owner's creativity. They reveal the tastes and personalities of the people who built them—and they are not for everybody. Floor plans are often eccentric and details may be idiosyncratic, such as no interior doors, a bathtub placed in the middle of living space, or considerable square footage in a prime location but only one bedroom and one bath. Such design extremes may lower resale value, but many artistic owner/builders are unconcerned because they plan to live in their masterpieces for the rest of their lives.

If you're considering building with straw bales as an artistic expression, address the question that Canadian architect Bruce Lockhart asks all his clients: In the future, if you have to sell your dream home, are you able to wait for a sale longer than usual? Investing in an unconventional home worth hundreds of thousands of dollars can be risky.

Assuming you're willing to take that risk, straw bales are an ideal material for making your unique vision a reality. Let this chapter inspire you, and create away!

Adjacent to the Los Padres National Forest in California, the Semmeses built their strawbale dream house to emulate a Santa Fe-style adobe.

Atascadero, California

For more than twenty years, busy contractor Turko Semmes has been creating custom homes near Atascadero, California. His company is known for quality construction of thick-walled buildings with an old-world look and the use of innovative twenty-first-century materials. It says a lot, then, that when it came to building a home for himself and his wife, BJ, he chose to build with straw bales.

BJ and Turko had been imagining their dream house for fifteen years, so they had a good idea of what they wanted. Lovers of Santa Fe and pueblo-style architecture, they incorporated deep window and door openings and niches into their design. They were already living in a compact home on their own land, so they created a spacious home for just the two of them and kept the existing place as their guesthouse.

BJ wanted plenty of natural light. Turko was concerned with passive solar orientation. He uses the mantra "orientation, insulation and mass" to explain to clients how he "designs houses to be warmer in winter, cooler in summer, and keep energy costs down." The result of their collaboration is energy efficiency invisibly integrated into their comfortable and stylish home.

The friendly kitchen/family room is where friends gather; they can either help or just watch as BJ and Turko whip up a gourmet meal. An operable skylight over the large, central butcher block floods light into the space. Through an arched doorway, the long dining and living room provides an elegant entertaining space. The wide interior walls mimic the thickness of the strawbale exterior walls and make space for custom-built buffets and storage. The east end houses the master bedroom and bath. On the west is office space. Turko raves, "The floor plan is fantastic. If more bedrooms were needed, they could be added on the office end."

Although they have ample acreage adjacent to the Los Padres National Forest, the Semmeses worked to keep a small footprint on the landscaped and built area, as they are participating in a native grass restoration project. They wanted the view from the bedroom, dining and living rooms to "feel like the outdoors was indoors." Turko accomplished this by berming the home into the slope about eighteen inches," which puts the five wide, south-facing window seats right at ground level on the outside. This provides them with an ever-changing wildlife show, as peacocks,

The fixed south-facing windows bring in light and heat, and offer daily views of wildlife feeding in the pasture and nearby forest.

foxes, red-tailed hawks, wild turkeys and deer, attracted by a rippling green meadow of perennial grasses, feed in their backyard daily.

Due to seismic concerns and the need to keep bales dry during construction, Turko chose to build a post-and-beam structure, infilled with rice straw bales from California's Central Valley. He followed up-to-date building techniques for earthquake-prone areas, eliminating pinning in favor of a bed of nails in the bottom plates, and two-by-two-inch woven wire mesh that securely ties the roof to the foundation. Turko enjoyed the process. "I love the synergy of many people with different levels of skill working together in a positive barn-raising atmosphere."

Turko kept the cost down on the custom south-facing view windows by limiting their overall size, and the effect is still stunning. An efficient Rumford fireplace in the living room backs up the hydronic radiant heat installed in the concrete floors, which are finished with an acid-etched stain that gives them an antique patina. A well-insulated ceiling topped with modified Bituthane roofing keeps the weather out; the low-sloped roof sports traditional *canales* (ceramic or metal channels for directing runoff water away from the walls). For better protection from the elements, Turko says in hindsight, "I would change the roof, which is a pueblo style with parapets, to a gable roof with overhangs."

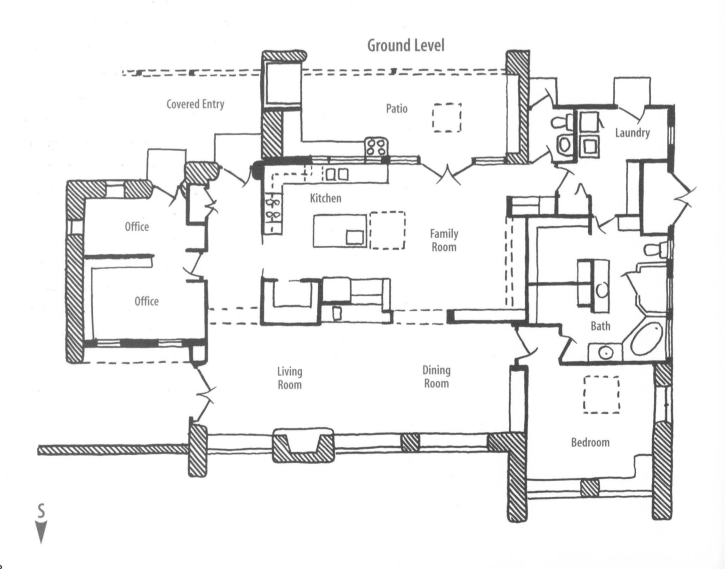

Ground Level

Covered Entry

Patio

Laundry

Kitchen

Office

Family Room

Office

Bath

Living Room

Dining Room

Bedroom

S

Elegant arches and thick interior walls mimic the arched window openings along the south wall. The deepness of the room dividers is utilized by built-in buffets in the dining and living rooms.

The custom cabinetry was fashioned from old-growth Douglas fir salvaged from bleachers at Cal Poly University (after sanding off the old bubblegum). Turko made their gorgeous dining table from local sycamore and the eaves from cypress trees blown down in the wind. Their fireplace mantel was crafted from California madrone burned in a Big Sur forest fire. A smooth gypsum plaster and low VOC paints complete their nontoxic interior.

After a year of construction, doing all the work themselves with the help of their college-age sons, the Semmeses moved in and BJ began decorating with art they collected during their travels—a hand-carved St. Francis from Santa Fe in a special niche, a Diego Rivera-style pressed-flower "painting" over the mantel, and family memorabilia. Her biggest concern during building was "trying to afford what we wanted. There is always that temptation to overspend the budget, and, of course, we did. I only wish the living room was five feet wider—we were trying to save on square footage."

Still, the final product showcases the Semmeses' ability to combine aesthetics and energy efficiency and has become their favorite example to share with future clients. Turko found the challenge of working together as husband and wife and making decisions on details and finishes as a positive experience. BJ concurs, "We're in heaven."

Square footage: 1,900 interior, 2,090 exterior
1 bedroom, 1 ½ baths + office, 1 story, post-and-beam
Architect: Owner-designed
Owner/builder: Semmes & Co Builders
Cost per square foot: $150

Perth, Ontario, Canada

The design for Wayne Skerritt and Joan Hughes' strawbale home sprang from their intuitive response to its location—a wooded lot overlooking a lake near Perth, Ontario. Their intention was that the house be in harmony with the site's geography, climate, sun and moon cycles, and the four directions.

After spending time on the property, Wayne felt that their site required a fluid-yet-stable design. "I was exploring the idea that different shapes have differing effects on our body and psyche. The square is unstable, the circle is fluid and moving, and the octagon has the qualities of both." With all this in mind, Wayne and Joan created a unique floor plan: a triad of interlocking octagons creating a dynamic and amazingly functional space.

The three octagonal pods meld together, overlapping at the center. The eastern pod reveals an open kitchen/dining/living space with a southern exposure. An identical pod on the west houses the master bedroom, guest bedroom and Wayne's office. In between, on the north, a half-pod is Joan's office and painting studio. A passageway joins the three, with a view out onto a spacious deck overlooking the lake below. Like a prism, windows at angles across the entire south-face bring in light and heat, and connect the space to its natural setting. Wayne offers, "We get up and go to bed with the sun. Living in harmony with the laws of nature is the central theme of the design."

This window ledge emulates the natural shape of wind-blown sand.

Small north-facing view windows open out for venting.

Wayne and Joan lived in a trailer on-site during construction, acting as general contractors. They hired four carpenters with expertise in all aspects of construction, and brought in subcontractors as necessary. With a background in architectural design, fine furniture building and home renovation, Wayne did as much as he could, while keeping track of the overall project. When they were ready to stack bales, friends and volunteers showed up to help out, and Wayne found himself being "teacher and learner at the same time." Wayne asserts, "The parging (stuccoing) is what gives the walls their strength and visual appeal. The moisture introduced by plastering will dry out over time and the wall will find a balance point of moisture."

The hall culminates into an octagonal space, where natural light enhances a pleasing combination of shape, color and texture.

A wooded lakeside near Perth, Ontario, offered a challenging site and a spectacular, secluded setting.

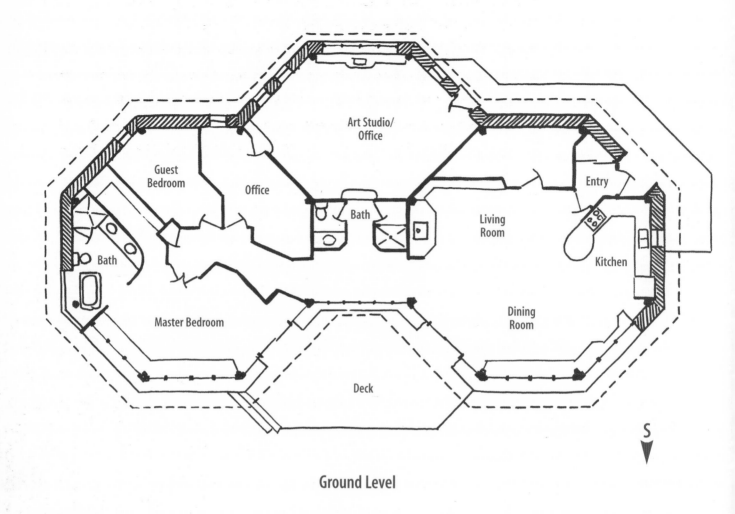

Ground Level

The slab-on-grade foundation ties into solid rock on the site. The corner posts for the octagonal pods were cast-in-place concrete, and their placement had to be very precise. Two-by-twelve-inch laminated wooden beams are mechanically tied to the posts and form the support for the roof structure over the pods. Trusses create the structure over the center section, and the roof is insulated with mineral wool batts and cellulose. Special skill was required to complete this compound roof and flash it correctly.

Despite the thermopane windows, the sheer expanse of glass reduces the home's overall energy-efficiency, especially in this northerly climate where solar gain is limited. So Wayne and Joan installed thermal blinds to insulate the window walls at night. The hydronic (radiant) floor heating system provides wintertime comfort, with a wood-fired boiler located in an out-building. Heating with wood, a plentiful local resource, has proven to be an economical choice.

Wayne and Joan consciously selected nontoxic paints and varnishes and other natural materials for their home's interior. They also incorporated art pieces, paintings and creative details throughout. One windowsill is hand carved from quarter-inch layers of pine to mimic the visual effect of wind-blown sand. Their friend and neighbor Greg Robinson designed and built a spiral stained-glass insert for the solid maple front door and adjacent window.

Joan and Wayne are pleased with their floor plan, although Wayne admits, "I would design more storage space and make the walk-in closet in the master bedroom wider." They remain enthusiastic about their choice to build with bales. Wayne says proudly, "The walls are very stable and the strawbales are as strong and dry as the day we put them up." He also advises, "Do your homework. Take your time during the design process and then go for it. You will never regret living in a strawbale house."

A sheltered south-facing deck makes a lovely outdoor living/dining room.

Square footage: 2,735 interior, 2,918 exterior
2 bedroom, 1 ½ bath, 1 story, post-and-beam
Architect: Owner-designed
Owner/builder (with professional help)
Approximate cost per square foot: $90 (Canadian)

East Meredith, New York

In the foothills of the Catskills, 170 miles (but a world away) from Manhattan, Clark Sanders has been quietly exploring the strawbale medium since he built the world's first "permitted" bale structure in 1989. A self-taught builder and now adjunct teacher at Hardwick College's ecological campus, he shares his knowledge of working with natural materials with his students, balancing idealism and pragmatism. Clark had to practice this balancing act himself in his latest construction, a handcrafted, high-end strawbale home built "on speculation."

On forty-five acres of unlogged hardwood forest with fieldstone-fenced pastures, Clark's new strawbale home stands high above the valley. With its steep-pitched roof, aged wooden beams and lime plaster, it could have been transplanted from old-world Europe. The design was based on guidelines from *A Pattern Language*, a classic architectural text from Christopher Alexander, and its evolution was a big part of the two-year building process.

The home is shaped to form a sheltered courtyard along the covered front entryway. Inside, a hall leads to a guest suite/study on the left and opens to a spacious kitchen/dining room on the right. A sweeping sculpted staircase leads to the three second-

LEFT: A glowing fire and sensual lines of a winding staircase give this unfinished room endless potential for personalizing the space. Note the "hobbit hole" at the base of the stairs.

BELOW: Hearkening to European traditions and A Pattern Language, designer/builder Clark Sanders wanted this home to feel historic from its inception.

floor bedrooms and also serves to visually separate the intimate kitchen from an elegant living room. The space beneath the stairway has a hobbit-like entry for children only (adults can access the room through a closet). Says Clark, "People respond positively to the design. And kids love the secret room. When they hear about it, they're in it quicker than lightning."

As the hill faces north, Clark positioned the house far enough down the slope to allow for passive solar gain. To choose the best views, he waited until the structure was up before finalizing window placement. While most of the home is finely finished, the kitchen and master bath were purposely left incomplete, awaiting input from the future owners. Clark comments, "The design process was a dance, and strawbale represented maybe 1 percent of it."

"Because of the volume of space and the mass of the larger walls, we chose a post-and-beam structure for the two-story part, while the single-story guest wing/study is load-bearing," says Clark. Bales were laid flat in the load-bearing walls, and on edge (for a narrower wall) in the post-and-beam section. Clark admits, "With load-bearing, the sequencing of building elements is complex. The benefit of post-and-beam design is having a roof over your head, especially in the Northeast, where on any given day it could rain."

A stained-concrete slab-on-grade was poured atop a rubble trench foundation with a perimeter grade beam, insulated with two inches of rigid foam. Clark experimented with a soil-cement floor using local clays in the guest suite/study, which turned out looking like burnished leather—but it was challenging to find the right mix. "Concrete is self-leveling; an earth floor is

not." Locally harvested and milled lumber, plus salvaged barn timber and siding, were aesthetically incorporated into the structure and trim details. Upstairs floors are hand-finished white pine with a stairwell of vintage hemlock. Says Clark, "If you use vintage wood, the material does a lot of the design work, and the result is more

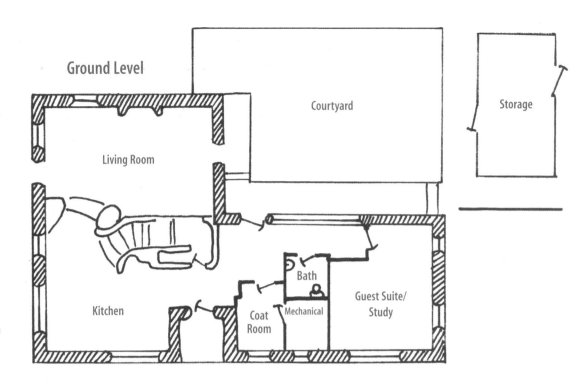

Ground Level

Courtyard

Storage

Living Room

Kitchen

Bath

Coat Room

Mechanical

Guest Suite/ Study

beautiful—though it does take more time and labor, collecting, sorting, storing, shaping and finishing. New lumber takes more design effort to make it sing."

Clark and his building partner, Tjalling Heyning, spared no effort and chose quality materials for this beautiful custom design. Double-paned, low-e, "architectural series" windows grace the south, east and north walls, while on the west triple-glazed windows with integral blinds mitigate excessive heat on summer afternoons. During the winter, in-floor radiant heat keeps the

Dormer windows add sunlight and usable space to a second-floor bedroom.

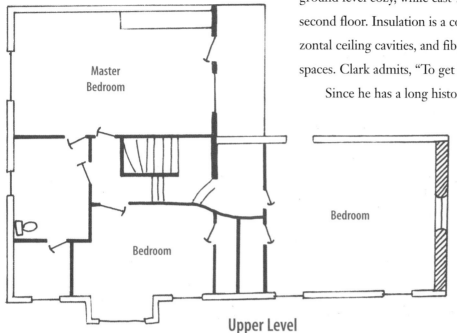

Upper Level

ground level cozy, while cast-iron baseboard and vintage radiators heat the second floor. Insulation is a combination of blown-in cellulose in the horizontal ceiling cavities, and fiberglass batts in the doghouse dormer vertical spaces. Clark admits, "To get R-49 insulation I had to overbuild the roof."

Since he has a long history of working with local building officials, Clark had no problems getting a permit. He ran electrical wire between the bales without any problems, making all connections in the boxes, per code. For plumbing he advises to avoid running pipes through the bale walls, to be sure there is plenty of access, and "make the access panels pretty."

His biggest concern was protecting all the surfaces throughout the lengthy building process. ("The finished floor is hard to keep nice.") In fact, the entire process is challenging. "The more complex the house, the more concerns. Making the edges crisp where dissimilar materials meet can be tricky. I always underestimate the time it takes."

As a life-long builder and now a teacher, Clark promotes sustainability, "Strawbale empowers people to get involved and enter into the building process, and like quicksand it sucks you in, and you can't get out. Straw bales are a perfect fit to my skills and beliefs."

Square footage: 2,700 interior, 3,000 exterior
4 bedrooms, 2 baths, 2 stories, post-and-beam/load-bearing
Designer: Clark Sanders, with Jessica Vernay
Builder: Clark Sanders and Tjalling Heyning
Cost per square foot: $150

The weathered barn-wood portal is supported by a decorative cast-concrete plinth.

Sonoma County, California

Annie Scully and Patricia Young knew exactly where they wanted to build their dream home: in the middle of a five-acre apple orchard in Sonoma County, California. According to Annie, "It was as if there was a sign posted there. It was indisputably the spot, and it has southern exposure and great views."

The two teachers hired Berkeley architect Darrell DeBoer. He came out for a brief on-site visit, listened to what the women wanted and drew a floor plan. "Literally, after just one good beer, we had conveyed and he had drawn what we now live in and are awed by," explains Patsy.

And awesome it is. The unique house features an expansive living room with high ceilings and a set of large bamboo doors that swing wide open to bring the outdoors in. The kitchen is adjacent to a glassed-in dining area with a view of the lap pool surrounded by apple trees. A staircase with handrails of madrone branches leads to a mezzanine bathroom with a balcony office that overlooks the living room. From there, Annie and Patsy climb a ladder to their sleeping loft. Softly undulating walls, a hand-sculpted fireplace, built-in *bancos*, oval windows, niches, natural wood accents and a handmade paper light fixture transform the unique floor plan into a bold artistic statement.

Scully and Young wanted to use as many recycled materials as possible. They felt good about straw bales as a way to use a waste product, and they knew the insulation factor would result in energy savings, so they built with bales of organic rice straw. Annie points out, "Truthfully, it was easy to be 'greener' because the final result with bales is always so warm. We accentuated their uneven surfaces, carved out niches and created curves. They are so sculptable, and when you are inside them, you feel the difference."

The foundation proved to be an expensive challenge because the orchard had been disked, so the soil was "disturbed." Although cement was the one material they didn't want to use, they were required to pour 36 pillars of reinforced concrete, each 11 feet deep and 1 foot in diameter.

Large south-facing windows embrace the view, protected by a curved overhang.

As in a fairytale, this whimsical strawbale home is set in the midst of an apple orchard.

They chose recycled corrugated material for the roof, blown-in cellulose ceiling insulation, double-glazed windows, earthen floors with radiant heat, lime plaster on the exterior and aliz plaster inside instead of paint.

Annie and Patsy lived in a trailer on-site during construction, which lasted exactly nine months. They moved in on winter solstice 2000. Ironically, it took longer to get the plans approved by the county than to build the house.

Their biggest challenge was respecting all the variables that working with people brings to the process, as well as trusting about things they didn't know and materials they'd never seen before. Their advice is to talk to people who've done it before and never approve any changes unless they are in writing with costs included, but they have high praise for their contractor and his crew. Patsy adds, "The architects and builders are artists who become like family. Like family, it's complicated and precious."

Square footage: 1,200 interior, 1,500 exterior
1 bedroom, 2 baths+ office, 1 ½ stories, post-and-beam
Architect: Darrel DeBoer
Builder: Tim Owen-Kennedy, Vital Systems
Cost per square foot: $230

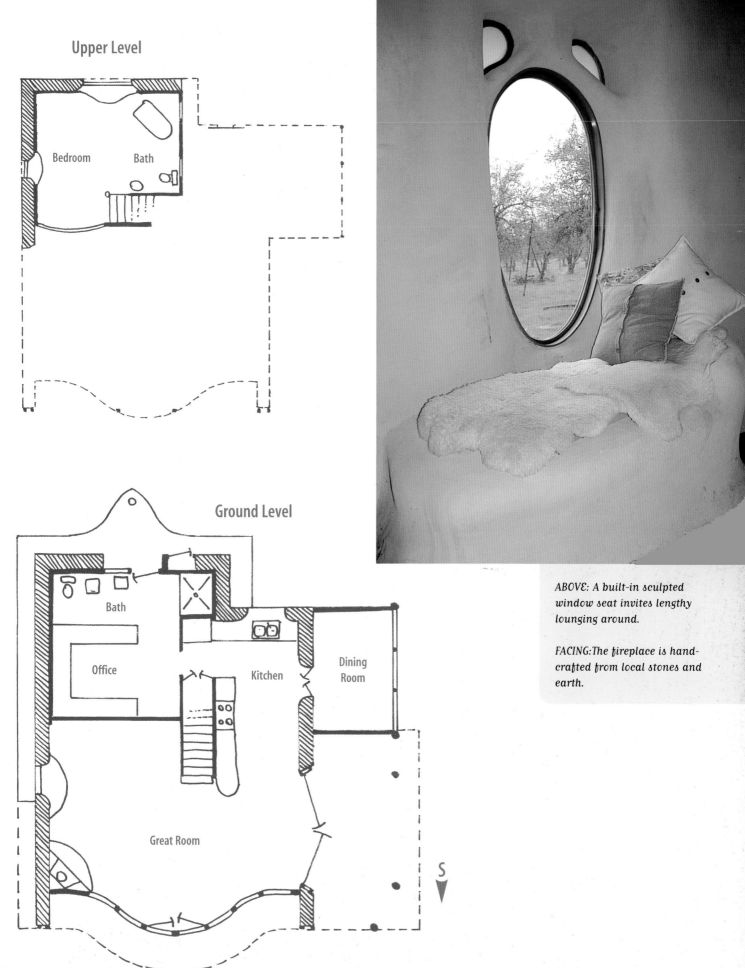

Upper Level

Bedroom Bath

Ground Level

Bath

Office

Kitchen

Dining Room

Great Room

S

ABOVE: A built-in sculpted window seat invites lengthy lounging around.

FACING: The fireplace is hand-crafted from local stones and earth.

Roaring Fork Valley, Colorado

The stress of building a house tests any couple's relationship, but Chris Bank and Paula Minnucci passed that test with flying colors. They designed and planned their strawbale home as a committed but unmarried couple. Then they wed on the site during construction and spent their honeymoon in the unfinished bedroom. Paula says, "This house brought me and Chris together."

Chris and Paula had very little building experience when they began to envision a home on their five-acre lot overlooking the Roaring Fork Valley, near Carbondale, Colorado. "We knew we wanted the roundness and softness of an adobe-style house," explains Chris, a musician and music teacher in the local schools. The space needed to function for their lives as a couple, yet occasionally host up to five of their grown children.

They also wanted healthy indoor air quality, serious insulation to weather the Colorado winters, and to keep costs low. Their ideas became reality with the help and guidance of Cedar Rose Guelberth, owner of the Building for Health Materials Center in downtown Carbondale. With Cedar Rose as designer and project manager, Chris and Paula became owner/builders, thus saving money by doing much of the labor themselves. The house was sited to take advantage of the southern exposure and a view of the meadow. Chris and Paula wanted the feeling of being tucked in rather than high and exposed, so the hillside was excavated to embrace the house, shed water and allow "energy to move around it," according to Cedar Rose. Construction began in 1996 and the newlyweds moved into their dream home in 1998.

With the goal of minimizing the use of energy-intensive cement, a concrete grade beam

was poured atop a three-and-a-half-foot-deep rubble trench, which also diverts moisture away from the home. They chose post-and-beam construction because, as Paula says, "The look of wooden beams is beautiful." Sustainably logged, windblown spruce trees were assembled into a timber frame utilizing traditional joinery (pegs only, no nails or metal plates) and then oiled with natural products. Cold seams—where the bale wall meets the timber frame—were carefully sealed or caulked to eliminate air infiltration. A whole-house ventilation system, recycled carpet and nontoxic carpet pads assure healthy indoor air. The house is completely "off the grid," with electricity provided by photovoltaic panels.

RIGHT: A wedding present for the homeowners, this sign suggests an attitude for all who pass within.

BELOW: Even a small entry room is a place to leave coats and muddy shoes, and create an air buffer against the cold.

The curved southwest corner creates an intimate area for dining, with an expansive view.

The simple square shape of the home is embellished with an air-lock entry and a curved southeast corner, designed to fit an heirloom dining table that belonged to Paula's mother. The open front family rooms are designed to welcome and nurture guests, while an arch that leads to the bedroom areas signifies sacredness and privacy. Their 400-square-foot loft was a result of selecting a Dutch hip roof, which allowed windows into what would have been attic space. Now visiting relatives can climb a ladder up to an antique-filled guest bedroom.

Interior walls are straw-clay infill or cob, which provides thermal mass and offers excellent soundproofing between rooms. Cozy seating areas are sculpted out of straw bales and cob, and poured-adobe floors feature radiant heat. Inside and outside, walls are finished with earth plasters colored with local clays and natural pigments that Paula and Chris applied themselves after intensive on-the-job training from Cedar Rose. Plasters were "keyed in" to the rough bale surface without the use of any metal wire or lath. The decorative stone facing at the base of the exterior walls also helps protect the earthen plaster from "splashback."

Paula and Chris slept in a tent on the site and often labored into the night by the light of their car headlights. Paula remembers, "We once worked for eighteen hours to insulate the attic, and we never got short or angry with each other." Because Chris had a basic background in construction, he felt the hands-on work was gratifying, but ultimately Chris and Paula both agree that the best part of the building process was completion.

According to Paula, "The greatest challenge was that it was so much work for the two of us. Fortunately, Chris was great at saying to me, 'Take it a day at a time,' . . . otherwise, it was too overwhelming. We've always liked the softness and curves of a strawbale home and using clean materials as well." Chris adds, "This house is like living inside a work of art."

Square footage: 1,780 interior, 1,800 exterior
3 bedrooms, 2 baths, 1 ½ stories, post-and-beam
Designer: Cedar Rose Guelberth
Owner/builders
Timber frame: Norm Luark, Magic Mesa Timberframe
Solar electric system: Scott Ely, Sunsence
Radiant floor heating: Mike Tierney, Aspen Solar
Approximate cost per square foot: $75

A cozy sculpted window seat graces the master bedroom.

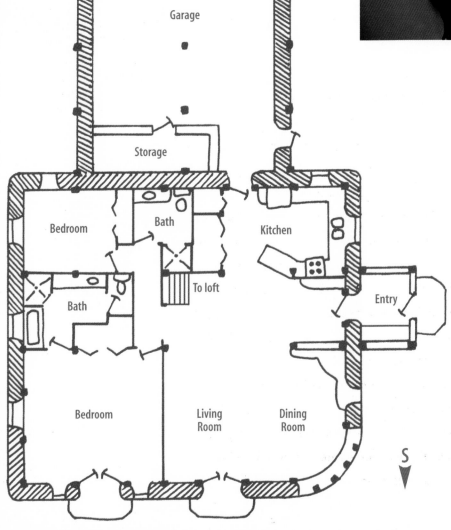

Lower Lake, California

As a healer, Linda Drew wanted her home to embody her commitment to holistic health for herself and the planet, and as an artist, she wanted her home to be a work of art. During her design process, Linda attended natural-building conferences, took classes and visited rammed earth, papercrete and cob structures. She became sold on strawbale when she walked into a small studio and went "ahhhh! It felt like I was being house hugged."

Linda met architect Pete Gang at a strawbale wall raising in northern California, "We talked and really connected with our philosophy and lifestyle beliefs." She described her vision of curves, color and lots of light. She told him she didn't want hard angles, hallways or doors and wanted to be "off the grid." Pete agreed to be her architect when she found her land.

Six months later, Linda bought a property in Lower Lake, California, the wine country between Calistoga and Harbin Hot Springs. She chose the area for its lush temperate climate, clean air (the cleanest in the state according to the EPA), like-minded people and proximity to the cultural life of San Francisco. Pete asked fellow architect Kelly Lerner to partner with him on the project. With Kelly and Pete's collaboration, Linda's vision became reality within one year.

Nestled into a knoll on thirteen acres of rolling hills dotted with oak trees, Linda's country home is the first permitted earth-plastered house in California. It's a work of art with coved ceilings, a curved cob bench around the dining table, sculpted *nichos*, a cob surround behind the wood stove and bas-relief plaster ornamentation on the walls. Linda's background as a ceramic artist served her well. She says, "My house was one big pot." Using natural pigments that gave her a rainbow of hues, she made all her paints by hand. Her bedroom is watery blue. The bathroom is soothing celadon. Her country French kitchen is bright yellow and cobalt blue, while the office is a dark, earthy brown.

The house faces south for passive solar gain and is bermed five feet into the earth on the north. The sun heats her water, and an array of photovoltaic panels supplies her electricity. A cooling tower keeps the house comfortable during sizzling summers; radiant floor heating and a wood stove warm the house during winter. A loft provides the perfect painting studio and space for overnight guests.

Code required cross-bracing the strawbale walls for seismic considerations. The three-string bales came from a rice farmer in California's Central Valley, less than an hour away. Cellulose, made from recycled waste paper, insulates the ceiling.

Although Linda hired various subcontractors, she was a hands-on owner/builder. She lived on the site in a trailer for the year that the house was under construction. Her workers—some of them young interns—camped on the land. She participated in every stage of the building and hosted workshops during the wall raising, cob building and plastering phases.

The inland valleys of California wine country experience hot summers, so design for comfort includes shade and air ventilation.

Skylights are particularly appreciated over the bath or shower area.

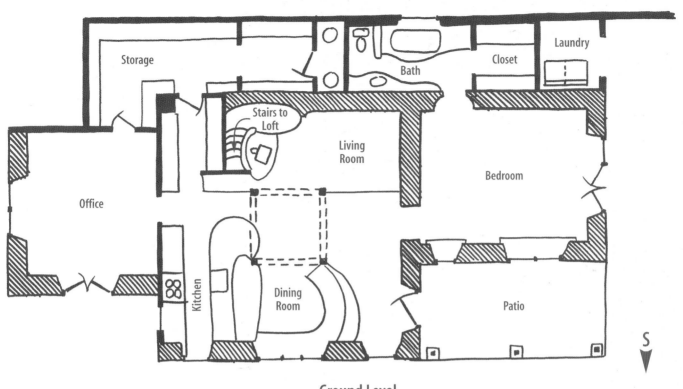

Ground Level

For Linda, the best part of building with bales was the wall-raising party, when twenty-five people showed up and the walls were completed in a weekend. Her greatest challenge was finding workers experienced in natural building and supervising novice workers. Linda advises, "Use experienced workers if you can find them, and keep it small and simple."

Square footage: 1,600 interior, 1,848 exterior
1 bedroom, 1 bath + office, 1 ½ stories, post-and-beam
Architects: Pete Gang, Common Sense Design and Kelly Lerner,
 One World Design
Owner/builder
Cost per square foot: $166

*A decorative nicho
by the front door.*

Aspen, Colorado

Peter Gina's dream home perches on the side of the Rocky
Mountains. The sophisticated bachelor enjoys views of
pristine wilderness from every window. Peter began his love
affair with nature when he worked ski patrol and lived in a
tiny rustic cabin with a sleeping loft that was open to the
stars. That cabin is the antithesis of the spacious, finely
detailed strawbale home he built near Aspen, Colorado, but
he still stargazes as he falls asleep in a loft with a skylight
revealing the sparkling constellations.

Originally from Manhattan's Upper East Side (where his
father was a commercial architect and his grandfather was the
proprietor of Sardi's), Peter is an art collector and wine con-
noisseur who works as a waiter in one of Aspen's most elegant
restaurants. He began designing his dream house six years
before breaking ground. He chose strawbale because "I like
the adobe look of thick walls with the recessed windows and
doors. I appreciate the insulation value and the earth-friendly
nature of the material."

Peter hired Carbondale architect Jeff Dickenson, who
designed the strawbale Waldorf School on the Roaring Fork.
Jeff says, "Peter is very meticulous. He has good taste and had
strong ideas about what he wanted. This was not going to be
a shack in the woods nor a typical Aspen estate. We had many
discussions about almost every aspect of the house."

Together they selected the site for the house, considering
the views, safety from wildfires and proximity to a pond and
aspen grove on Peter's 100-plus acres. They decided to orient
the house on the east/west axis for maximum solar gain. Peter
and Jeff created an ambitious plan, including improving the
road to get supplies and equipment to the building site. Straw
bale walls went up during weekend gatherings of Peter's
friends and students from nearby Solar Energy International.

According to Jeff, "I think the building process was even more interesting for Peter. . . .
Toward the end, he said to me, 'I've learned not to get upset at every little problem. Problems
can be fixed.' This was after an excavator had cut through the power line leading from his PV
panels to his house."

Sunset in the Rocky Mountains bathes the landscape in a magical light.

LEFT: An oval view window invites wildlife watching.

RIGHT: A special tree becomes a structural post and adds beauty to the interior space.

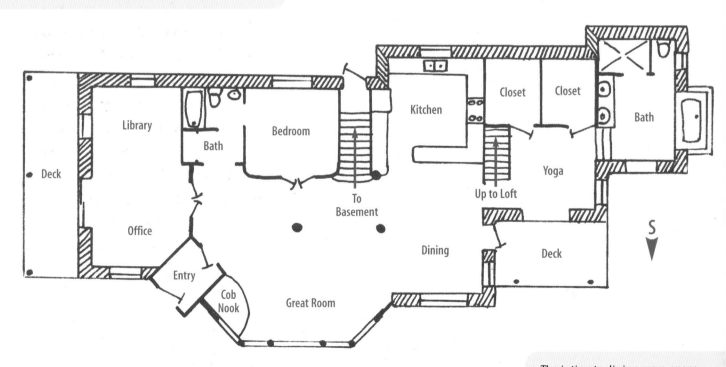

The intimate dining room opens into a light-filled great room.

The finished house reflects its owner's appreciation for quality and beauty. The cozy entrance foyer opens into a grand great room with cathedral ceilings and a wall of windows revealing breathtaking views of the Rocky Mountains. An intimate dining room adjoins a spacious modern kitchen. The east end houses a room just for yoga, and the master bath boasts a sunken tub with an awesome view of the mountains to the north. Decks on the southeast and northwest are made of salvaged redwood and logs harvested from trail cutting. A darkroom is tucked into a partial basement.

The remote location of Peter's home necessitates being "off the grid." Electricity is supplied by a PV system, and solar panels preheat domestic hot water. The foundation and basement level were created with ten-inch insulated concrete forms (ICFs) filled with reinforced concrete. Truss joists above the ICFs support a three-inch concrete slab containing radiant-heat tubing. The exposed, handcrafted timber frame combines round posts with rough-cut rafters. No paint was used in the house. Instead, wood surfaces were treated with natural wood preservatives and bales were plastered with a smooth gypsum finish. Straw/clay was used to create curved interior walls, and a hand-sculpted cob reading nook graces a corner of the great room.

Peter's biggest concerns during building were the proper alignment of bale walls and their structural integrity. He also worried about the quality of the stucco. Now he says, "I am pleased with the floor plan, and I do like the results so far." Jeff points out that the cost of building with bales is about the same as conventional building, "you just get a better product." He's noticed that owners of strawbale homes tend to get more involved in the building process, "when they are doing a strawbale, there's a buzz about it."

Today, every wall displays fine art, antique photographs of the American West and objets d'art acquired on foreign travels, yet Peter insists that his house "is still very much a work in progress. The heating system and solar electricity need tweaking, and there's more landscaping and interior decorating to come." His advice to others: "Do things that are funky and express your likes. Make your home yours."

Square footage: 2,689 interior, 3,099 exterior
2 bedrooms, 2 baths + office, 1 story with sleeping loft and
    basement, post-and-beam
Architect: Jeff Dickenson
Builder: Curtis Schieb
Solar electrician: Pat Kiernan
Approximate cost per square foot: $150

A sculpted cob wall creates a private reading/sleeping nook.

The alpine setting offers a
respite from urban stress.

Country Comfort

Building a home in the country is a postmodern American dream for which strawbale can be an ideal match. With room to spread out, the relative thickness of bale walls is not an issue, solar orientation is generally easy, and codes and covenants are typically more relaxed. This allows for more flexible floor plans and designs that invisibly incorporate energy efficiency into a low-maintenance home. Often, wood is a local resource, and passive solar strawbale buildings can function well with wood-fired heat.

Country homes are often designed to connect indoor and outdoor space through view windows, decks and patios. At the same time, landscape walls of bales (or other materials) can define the perimeter of the living area, protecting humans from wild creatures and vice versa. The clean air, peace and quiet, and reduced-stress lifestyle has value that can't be calculated.

However, building remotely has drawbacks. It will cost more to get utilities and transport materials to the site. Unless you have good local craftsmen, it will be more expensive to get workers, too.

Still, building in the country can be ideal for the self-reliant owner/builder. Taking your time and paying as you go can result in mortgage-free living, which means freedom to follow your muse. If you can arrange to telecommute or create your own home/Internet-based business, you'll be around more to enjoy the simple pleasures of country living. It just may turn out to be the life you've dreamed of.

Drought-tolerant species and a shallow pool provide a lush landscape in a dry microclimate. (Van Cleve Residence, Yakima, Washington)

Crestone, Colorado

For Kaia Derkum and David Woodward, building a strawbale home in the San Luis Valley of Colorado was a family affair. Her grandparents had owned a summer home near Crestone for decades, so when Kaia and David started looking for land, it was a logical choice. The family home provided a place to live in while they built their own house, with ample help from brothers, sisters, in-laws and Kaia's parents, who had significant building skills. Says Kaia, "Working with our family was the best part of the process. They were all able to join in because the materials provided an easy learning curve."

As owner/builders, Kaia, a fiber artist and painter, and David, a photographer, took about two years to complete their home and move in, but this do-it-yourself perseverance paid off handsomely in money saved. Now they own their new home free and clear.

David's background is in mechanical engineering and physics, so his understanding of the systems and attention to detail served them well. To him, the perfect solar-house design is based on the "holy trinity"—super insulation, solar orientation and thermal mass inside the insulated envelope. On the site they called him "Mr. R-value," as he was so particular about everything from foundation to attic insulation and sealing air gaps and cold joints. Kaia is not complaining: "We have lived very happily for six years in our strawbale house without a furnace." They do have a woodstove, which they fire up about twice a week during the winter.

They used computer software to model the solar design, which benefits from the abundant southwestern sunlight. A "greenbelt" adjacent to their land gave them flexibility to orient the house for solar and views. They also selected a site that is away from wildlife corridors. Consulting with local designer/builder Peter May, who is experienced with strawbale, David and Kaia worked on their floor plan over the winter, and started building in the spring.

A wide porch on the north keeps snow away from the carved wooden front door, and an air-lock mudroom entry seals the winter wind out. Inside, a low ceiling created by their upstairs art studios opens into a tall living room. Also on the south is their cozy kitchen with great views. A spacious bedroom takes up the southeast end of the L-shaped design, and a long, narrow bathroom connects the rooms along the north wall. Hand carvings over all the doorways complement the rustic interior finish, which is furnished with handsome antiques—gifts from Kaia's treasure-hunting aunts. "Overall we're pleased with the floor plan. We would add another bath in the space where we now have one large bath, and maybe a guest bedroom."

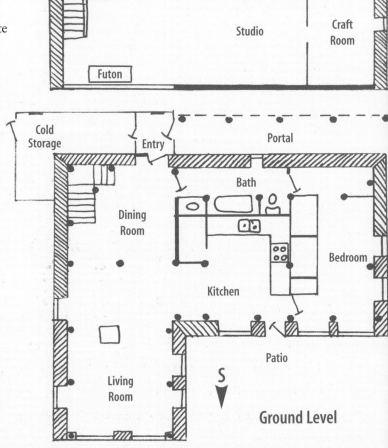

Upper Level

Studio

Craft Room

Futon

Cold Storage

Entry

Portal

Bath

Dining Room

Kitchen

Bedroom

Living Room

Patio

S

Ground Level

The foundation—a tall, concrete grade beam with an insulating pumice core—elevates the straw eighteen inches above the ground. This is much higher than code requires, but David was concerned about snow piling up against the bale walls. Floors are sandstone on sand, on top of eighteen inches of pumice as an insulating layer. A wood frame supports the metal roof with R-60 fiberglass insulation.

"With our two-story design and wide rooms, it seemed prudent to use a post-and-beam structure," says Kaia. "We chose strawbale because of the potential to achieve super insulation without double framing, and the walls can be put up fast." Still, David found it challenging to actually make all his engineering details come together during construction. Despite the joys of working with loved ones, Kaia found that her biggest challenge was "maintaining calm when we had different opinions on how to do things."

Plastering with cement/ lime stucco outside and gypsum inside, Kaia and David used wire mesh only around windows and doors. They placed all the plumbing in the core of the building, and the electrical wiring is largely inside interior walls or false beams, or around the foundation. Due to their supertight construction, they found significant vapor condensation indoors during cold weather, so after a couple years they installed a heat-recovery ventilator to reduce moisture buildup and bring in fresh air during the winter.

Impressed with the design and energy savings, Kaia's parents and brother are now building their own strawbale homes in the neighborhood, with Kaia and David as their number-one consultants.

ABOVE: Thick bale walls anchor a house in a vast landscape.
Photo by Bill Ellzey

LEFT AND BELOW: A portal along the north side offers shade in the summer and snow protection in the winter.

Square footage: 1,800 interior, 2,000 exterior
1 bedroom, 1 bath + studio, 1 ½ stories, post-and-beam
Architect: Owner-designed, consulted with Peter May, Earth Dance Design
Owner/builder
Approximate cost per square foot: $37

Coeur d'Alene, Idaho

Kathleen Barrett's strawbale home stands on the southern shore of Lake Coeur d'Alene in Idaho. Serene views of the placid lake dominate her spacious, light-filled great room and peaceful bedrooms. She accidentally stumbled on photographs of strawbale homes, and "it was love at first sight. I loved the organic lines and the non-machine-made look. Strawbale construction offered the possibility of creating a house that was literally 'handmade'."

A newspaper article led her to ecological architect Bruce Millard, and together they evolved the plan to build Kathleen's home as part of a duplex; the second unit will ultimately be a vacation home for her daughter's family on the lakefront land held in a family trust.

The house is bermed into the hill on the north and set on a foundation of Rastra block filled with concrete. Post-and-beam construction with non-milled log posts prevented bales from being rained on during building and allowed the installation of lots of windows in order to take advantage of priceless views.

The front entrance to the house opens onto the second floor. The inviting great room features cathedral ceilings, clerestory windows, glistening cherry floors, organic bale walls and a spectacular view of the lake. Adjacent is an intimate kitchen with restored antique cupboards and salvaged marble countertops, and a curved dining area housed in a Rastra turret. On the lower level, Rastra walls frame views of the lake from two bedrooms and a master bath. Windows on the lower level are covered by an arbor that provides shade in summer but doesn't block the sun in winter.

Kathleen found the best part of building with bales was the opportunity to have fun with shapes and finishes. "It was like creating a sculpture to live in." Her greatest challenges were cost overruns and a schedule that stretched to double the original estimate. "Some of the trade contractors were completely unprepared to do anything unusual or adapt their methods to a different type of construction. I'd advise anyone doing a strawbale house to *insist* on a pre-construction meeting of all trades and vendors so they know what they are getting into, and so the owner/builder can weed out ones who don't like it."

Square footage: 1,670 interior, 1,980 exterior
2 bedrooms, 2 baths, 2 stories, post-and-beam
Architect: Bruce Millard
Approximate cost per square foot: $130

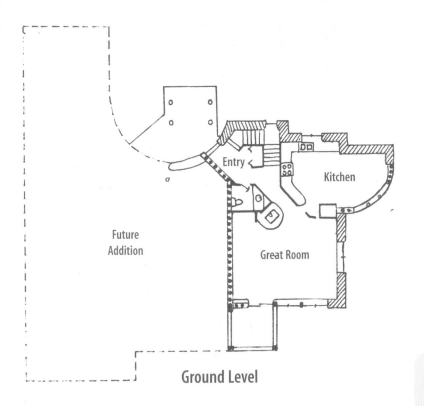

Ground Level

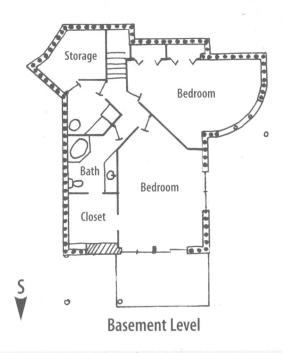

Basement Level

S

UPPER FACING: A compact dining room is adorned with hand-polished plasters.
BELOW FACING: An ideal lakeside lot provides earth-sheltering on the north and views to the south.
BELOW: A great room with a truly great view.

Balfour, British Columbia, Canada

Since moisture is the main enemy of strawbale construction, the rainforest of the Pacific Northwest is an extremely challenging climate for building with bales. Yet among the picturesque Kootenay Lakes near Balfour, British Columbia, architect Bruce Lockhart met the challenge of heavy snowfall and combined precipitation from rain and snow totaling about 28.7 inches a year. "It was a fun project," he says, "and one of my all-time favorite jobs."

Bruce designed a southwestern-style house for owner/builders Ron and Cher Watkins. They hired Habib Gonzalez, a regional builder who specializes in strawbale building, to help with construction. Eventually, they sold it to move back to their hometown and buy a winery. The current owner is Bill Harding, an American telecommuter who summers in British Columbia and winters in Tucson. Bill raves, "It's a great house, the best I've ever owned. The Watkinses did a great job, and I feel very lucky to have been able to buy it."

In siting the home, Bruce considered not only the fabulous view and southern exposure but also access in winter and ease of excavation. He gave special attention to designing the roof to carry a heavy snow load, protecting the walls from precipitation, and getting the approval of a building inspector who was very skeptical about the strawbale system. Overhangs were increased from twenty-four to thirty-six inches, and a post-and-beam structure was chosen for greater strength in supporting roof truss spans and snow loads of eighty pounds per square foot. The building inspector and mortgage lender were more comfortable with post-and-beam because they felt that if the bale walls failed, they could be replaced with another type of infill.

Flagstone steps lead up to the north-facing entrance. Straight ahead is the great room, with twenty-foot-high ceilings and exposed weathered timbers. The master bedroom suite is on the

LEFT: This Y-shaped design maximizes south and eastern exposure, in a northern climate.

FACING: Flagstone steps and the round timber frame create a dramatic front entry.

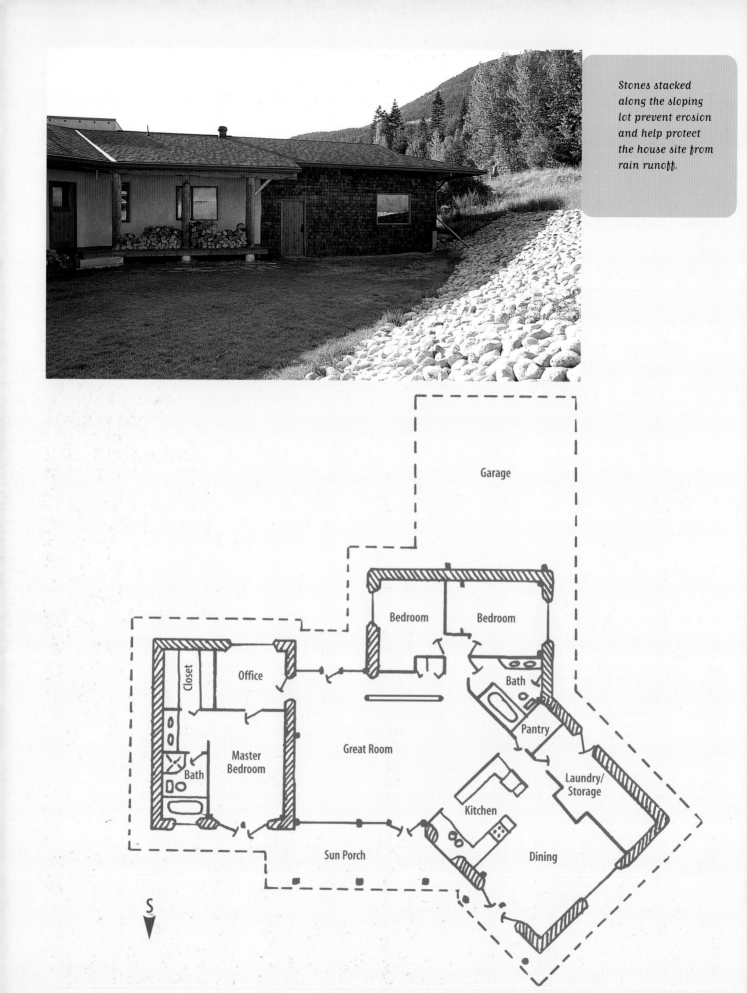

Stones stacked along the sloping lot prevent erosion and help protect the house site from rain runoff.

Garage

Bedroom

Bedroom

Closet

Office

Bath

Pantry

Bath

Great Room

Master Bedroom

Laundry/ Storage

Kitchen

Sun Porch

Dining

S

west, and two more bedrooms are to the east. The "gathering room" is a multipurpose kitchen/dining/sitting area—a pleasing juxtaposition of contemporary appliances and locally crafted birch furniture. The Y-shaped floor plan maximizes passive solar gain. Covered porches create outdoor living areas on the south and east sides of the house.

Gonzalez installed moisture monitors during construction in 1997, as part of a Canada-wide study. Relative humidity levels in all the walls have remained well within tolerances since the beginning, despite the moist climate of this temperate rainforest. After four years, an additional sensor was installed where there was a roof leak in a complex connection between the kitchen and living room. Recounts Habib, "A private building inspector and I drilled into the plaster and probed three sites on the wall. The highest reading was 26 percent immediately after the leak was discovered. The roofing contractor quickly repaired the flashing problem and the wall dried to 15 percent within two months."

Harding has spent two summers putting on finishing touches, enclosing the carport to create a garage, and landscaping. Because the custom-made windows and doors shrank and all had gaps of up to three-eighths inch, they had to be adjusted for a tight seal. But such concerns

French doors off the master bedroom bring in light and heat and offer a peerless view.

are minor compared to the pleasure the house gives him. He explains, "One must live in the strawbale house for a while to feel the spiritual quality it has, the quietness. I love the log posts and beams that also add a very special feel to the house."

Square footage: 2,018 interior, 2,240 exterior
3 bedrooms, 2 baths, 1 story, post-and-beam
Architect: Bruce Lockhart
Strawbale consultant: Habib Gonzalez, Sustainable Works
Approximate cost per square foot: Not available

A rustic dining area flows into a contemporary kitchen.

LEFT: Stone and wood combine to make a striking entryway.

Moscow, Idaho

When Steve and Marilyn Kohler brought designer and builder Kurt Rathmann to their property in the woods outside Moscow, Idaho, Kurt's first impression was, "No way!" No spot on their five acres was flat, and the only place with access was up a steep slope. But the Kohlers were so excited and positive about building their strawbale home on this site that Kurt took it on as a challenge, thinking, "This is a first; let's do it!"

Thus began a comfortable collaboration between owners and designer/builder, characterized by smooth communication and a professional yet personal relationship. Marilyn was passionate about the aesthetic of thick, curved, bale walls and wanted her home to be soothing and nurturing, with a "living feeling." She also wanted abundant windows and skylights to experience the forest surrounding them and to fill the house with light. When Kurt explained how too much "glazing" would seriously impact the energy efficiency of the structure, Marilyn made her selections thoughtfully.

Even with the compromises, the Kohler home has windows on every wall, and five skylights. The house is dug into the steep hill, ascending it with four levels of living space. The front door opens to a formal entry with stairs that lead to a living room with a floor-to-ceiling view into tall trees. A few more steps up is the open kitchen/dining room, where a door opens to a covered cedar deck with a hot tub and "wow" views. A short hall leads past a bath, to the library/guest room. Up another flight of stairs is the family/craft room, two bedrooms and a bath—and yes, they all have great views.

Working and building on the steep slope was the greatest challenge, and it also increased costs. An engineer was required for the foundation design as well as to calculate lateral loads on the bale walls. Rastra block, made from recycled Styrofoam and cement and filled with reinforced concrete, was chosen to create an insulating stem wall to support the bales. Outside, curved landscape and retaining walls are also sculpted and stuccoed Rastra block. The deck is supported by concrete piers that go deep down to bearing-soil strata. Floors are concrete, slate and wood—much of it salvaged and refinished.

Kurt, a young professional, acted as project manager for the official contractor, who handled payroll, insurance, etc. Kurt coordinated the complex schedule as the crew worked its way up the hill, pouring the various foundation walls and building the structural timber framework. Bales were delivered after the roof was on; three bale conveyors lifted them up to the second level, where they were stored out of the weather. The bale-raising stretched out over several weeks, benefiting from various

A meandering path takes
some of the steepness out
of this hillside lot.

volunteers interested in gaining hands-on experience.

Steve and Marilyn visited the site often, getting involved where they could in the construction process. Steve enjoyed working with the straw bales and Marilyn's job was to design all the
niches. They also worked closely with local chain saw artist Ted Kelchner, who created an
interior structural post that now graces their living room as a work of art. Steve was part of the
crew for the difficult and gratifying task of hoisting it into place.

Plastering a bale wall by hand is always a major process, and the Kohler home was no
exception. Thick coats of plaster inside and out evened out the bumps in the bales, resulting in
a smooth, undulating finish. Custom details include a stained-glass window, bookshelves,
cabinets, and lots of tile. As is typical, work went slower than planned, and after nearly six
months of construction, Kurt and his crew worked seven days a week so Steve, Marilyn, and
their son, Nathan, could move in before Christmas. Even with the pressure on, relationships

*Organic shapes soften
walls and direct flow
through the vertical space.*

remained cordial, and final finishing touches were completed with the Kohlers in residence. Marilyn would make just one change, "We would put the mechanical room in the basement storage area. It is noisy."

When building a home among the trees, the threat of forest fire must be addressed. Fortunately, a metal roof and straw bales covered with stucco are virtually fireproof. The Kohlers also chose to face some of the outside walls with corrugated steel material that matches the roof. In addition, Kurt positioned the septic drain field below the home to act as a firebreak from flames racing up the hill. Now the Kohlers' chief vulnerability is their wooden deck, so they have cleared the undergrowth and selectively cut trees to limit fire potential on that side of the house.

The steel siding and pale pink stucco give the home's exterior a very contemporary look. And inside, the play of natural light across soft surfaces evokes the spiritual feeling Marilyn and Steve were seeking.

Square footage: 2,300 interior, 2,600 exterior
2 bedrooms, 2 baths + library, 4 levels, post-and-beam
Designer/builder: Kurt Rathmann, 3 Little Pigs Design-Build
Engineer: Eric Hasenoehrl, Progressive Engineering
Contractor: Mark Hume, Hume Builders, Inc.
Approximate cost per square foot: $100

FACING: Large south-facing picture windows allow light and heat into the living room.

BELOW: A difficult site, but the view is worth it.

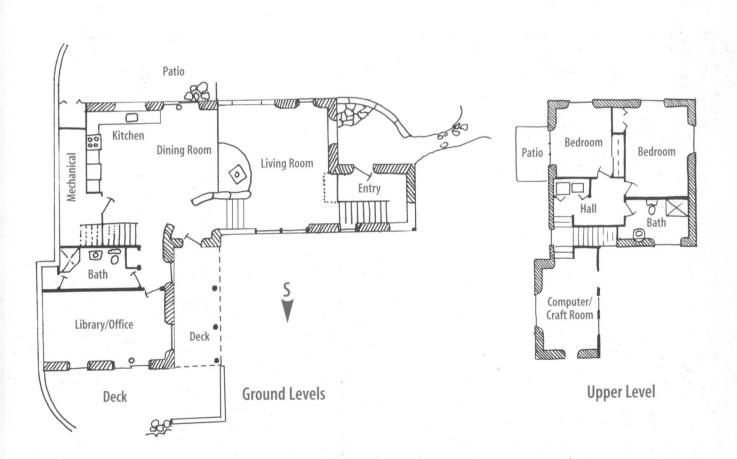

Patio

Kitchen

Dining Room

Living Room

Mechanical

Entry

Bath

S

Library/Office

Deck

Deck

Ground Levels

Patio

Bedroom

Bedroom

Hall

Bath

Computer/
Craft Room

Upper Level

Durango, Colorado

Sometimes you create your own synchronicity. If you are clear about what you want and do your homework, you just might get the home you're dreaming about. That's how it went for Tom Bartels and Jennie Dear, who, while hiking across their land near Durango, Colorado, and visualizing the strawbale home they planned to build on the site, bumped into John Fitzpatrick and asked him what he did for a living. "I'm a strawbale builder," he grinned.

Tom had been thinking about green building for at least a decade, having helped build rammed earth and strawbale homes, and as a producer of environmental educational videos, including one called *Sustainable Architecture*. After meeting his wife-to-be, Jennie Dear, a professor at Ft. Lewis College, they began planning in earnest to move out of their drafty rental in downtown Durango and build a home in a quieter, more natural location.

Tom and Jennie designed the floor plan together on their computer, using 3-D Architect software, which allowed them to see a virtual model of their design. They had common tastes and found it easy to agree. Over time they saved a

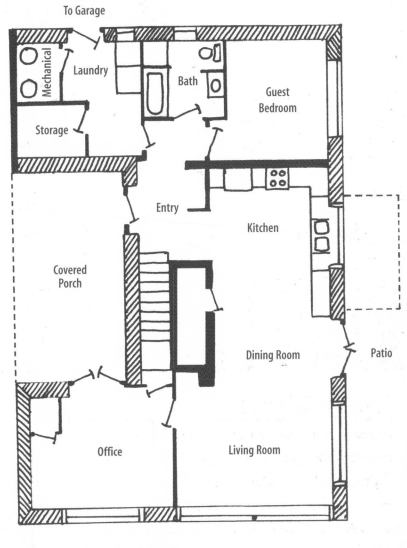

Ground Level

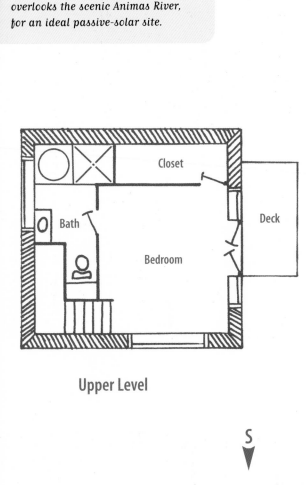

Upper Level

notebook of clippings of home ideas that they showed to their builder, John Fitzpatrick, to illustrate what they liked. The collaboration resulted in the home they had dreamed of. "We love strawbale and would not change a thing," asserts Jennie.

Transplanted from Scotland, Fitzpatrick grew up practicing old-world craftsmanship and brought that building ethic to his contracting business in Colorado. He believes strawbale construction is well suited to the local heating/cooling climate, and found that the challenge was structural support of the high snow-load potential. John remembers "lots of meetings with Tom and Jennie to discuss how to minimize impact and preserve the site." He explains that the floor plan was designed to maximize the indoor/outdoor room effect—à la *A Pattern Language*, by Christopher Alexander.

The house is approached from the west through an adobe landscape wall, where flagstones lead to a covered porch. Just inside, a built-in "entry center" is an organizational desk/cabinet,

Great room arch—the open floor plan makes the most of modest square footage.

with a place to drop a briefcase, hang a coat, leave a message, etc. Through an arched doorway is a spacious kitchen/dining/living room, with windows to the east and south. French doors provide easy access to a covered deck and, just yards away, a spectacular cliff-side view of the Animas River, two hundred feet below.

A wheelchair-accessible guest suite on the north does double duty as the screening room, keeping the TV out of common space. A laundry and large storage room fill out the north side. On the south is a roomy home office with more French doors open to the front porch.

ABOVE: The home office has a separate entry from the covered front porch.

FACING: An arched entryway frames the view into the kitchen.

Upstairs, the master bedroom features a durable bamboo hard-wood floor, and a deck overlooking the river to the southeast. This room has it all—light, solar heat, ventilation and views—and a serene feeling. The compact master bath features a Japanese soaking tub and "hers and his" shower heads.

John consulted with an engineer to create structural drawings that required minimal changes to the plan Tom and Jennie drew. From the insulated foundation to the pro-panel roof, the home was crafted with quality nontoxic materials—including Saltillo tile and bamboo floors, non-VOC paint, and custom cabinets from old bleacher seats salvaged from the Durango fairgrounds. Everyone remembers the highlight of the process as the wall-raising, when fifty friends of Tom and Jennie's showed up to help stack the bales. All the strawbale walls were built in a single, festive weekend.

Getting the design right has paid off in energy savings and comfort. A standard water heater, not a boiler, reduces mechanical and operating costs for their hydronic heat. "Radiant floors are great in winter. And during the summer we don't need air-conditioning," says Jennie. Still, after the experience of building this home, John advises, "Allow for extra time over conventional construction."

About a year after building began, Jennie and Tom were married on their land and hosted a wedding reception for a hundred friends in their just-completed home. Today, their beautiful and functional home reflects their values and provides support to their busy lifestyle. Their advice for others interested in building with bales is, "Go for it!" . . . And they lived happily ever after.

Square footage: 1,803 interior, 2,156 exterior
2 bedrooms, 2 baths + office, 1 ½ stories, post-and-beam
Architect: Owner-designed
Builder: John Fitzpatrick, Highland Fabricators, LLC
Approximate cost per square foot: $130

Resources

Architects/Designers

Anni Tilt, David Arkin
Arkin-Tilt Architects
Berkeley, California
510.528.9830
www.arkintilt.com

Michel Bergeron
Archibio
Montreal, Quebec, Canada
514.985.5734
www.archibio.qc.ca

Wayne J. Bingham, Architect
Salt Lake City, Utah
801.557.4212
www.wjbingham.com

Kari Bremer
Natural & Green Design
Durango, Colorado
970.946.8555
www.naturalgreendesign.com

Linda Chapman, Architect
Ottawa, Ontario, Canada
613.231.4690
www.smartarchitecture.com

Darrel DeBoer, Architect
Alameda, California
510.865.3669
www.deboerarchitects.com

Jeff Dickenson, Architect
Energy and Sustainable Design
Carbondale, Colorado
970.963.0114
www.energyandsustainabledesign.com

Ed Dunn
Solar Design & Construction
Flagstaff, Arizona
928.774.6308
solared@gmail.com
http://web.mac.com/solardc

Pete Gang, Architect
Common Sense Design
Petaluma, California
707.762.4838
www.commonsensedesign.com

Robert Gay, Architect
Radius Architects, LLC
Tucson, Arizona
520.575.8239
www.radius-architects.com

Cedar Rose Guelberth, Designer
Building For Health Eco Center
Carbondale, Colorado
970.963.0437
www.buildingforhealth.com

Ken Haggard, Polly Cooper & Scott Clark, Architects
San Luis Sustainability Group
Santa Margarita, California
805.438.4452
www.slosustainability.com

Tom Hahn RA/LC
Ecosa Design Studio
Prescott, Arizona
928.541.1002
www.EcosaDesign.com

Martin Hammer, Architect
Berkeley, California
510.525.0525
mjhammer@pacbell.net

Sigi Koko
Down To Earth
Bethlehem, Pennsylvania
610.868.6530 or 202.302.3055
www.buildnaturally.com

Kelly Lerner, Architect
One World Design
Spokane, Washington
509.838.8812
www.one-world-design.com

Bruce Millard, Architect
Studio of Sustainable Design
Sandpoint, Idaho
208.263.3815
www.bemarchitect.com

Benjamin Obregon, Architect
The Sustainable Design Center
Austin, Texas
512.263.0177
www.SustainableDesignCenter.com

Terry Phelan, Architect
Living Shelter Design
Issaquah, Washington
425.427.8643 or 888.248.2114
www.livingshelter.com

Touson Saryon
Integral Design Studio
Mt. Shasta, California
530.918.9370
www.IntegralDesignStudio.com

Daniel Mathew Silvernail, Architect
Soquel, California
831.462.9138
www.silvernailarch.com

Charles Simon, Architect & Planner
Eden Mills, Ontario, Canada
519.856.9921
www.simon-archplan.com

Daniel Smith, Dietmar Lorenz
Daniel Smith and Associates
Berkeley, California
510.526.1935
www.dsaarch.com

Howard Switzer and Katey Culver
Ecoville ArchiTects
Linden Tennessee
931.589.6513
http://earthandstraw.com

Karlis Viceps, Designer, Consultant
Energyscapes
Taos, New Mexico
575.770.0225
www.solarplans.com

Builders

Laura Bartels
Greenweaver, Inc.
Carbondale, Colorado
970.379.6779
www.greenweaverinc.com

Alan Bernholtz
Wind River Timberframes
Mancos, Colorado
970.822.2112
www.windriver-timberframes.com

Bob Bolles
Sustainable Building Systems
Poway, California
858.486.6949
www.strawbalehouse.com

Habib John Gonzalez
Sustainable Works
Crescent Valley, B.C., Canada
250.359.5095
www.sustainableworks.ca

Mark Hoberecht
HarvestBuild Associates, Inc.
Columbia Station, Ohio
440.236.3344
www.harvestbuild.com

Tim Owen-Kennedy
Vital Systems - General Contractor
Ukiah, California
888.859.6336
www.vitalsystems.net

Paul Koppana
Skyhawk Construction
Crestone, Colorado
719.256.4505
paulkoppana@hotmail.com

Michele Landegger & Debrae Lopes
Boa Constructor Building & Design
Watsonville, California
408.848.1117
www.buildingnaturally.com

Frank Meyer
Thangmaker Construction
Austin, Texas
512.517.9272
www.thangmaker.com

Ben Polley
Harvest Homes
Ontario, Canada
866.231.1100
www.harvesthomes.com

Kurt Rathmann
Rathmann Design, Inc. and
3LP Builders, Inc.
Spokane, WA 99204
509.389.4886
rathdesign@comcast.net

Jon Ruez
Tucson, Arizona
520.360.3646
jcruez@mac.com

Clark Sanders
Just Another Way Builder
East Meredith, New York
607.278.5144

Curtis Scheib
Eco Energy Builders
Salida, Colorado
970.948.2747
www.ecobuilders.com

Turko Semmes
Semmes & Co Builders, Inc.
Atascadero, California
805.466.6737
www.semmesco.com

Tina Therrien, Chris Magwood, Peter Mack
Camel's Back Construction
Madoc, Ontario, Canada
www.strawhomes.ca

Trey Warren
Whimpy Wolf Builders
Lander, Wyoming
307.349.2023
www.WhimpyWolf.com

Cadmon Whitty
Paja Construction, Inc.
Albuquerque, New Mexico
505.345.4843 or 505.306.2529
cadmonwhit@aol.com

Consultants

Andy Mueller
GreenSpace Collaborative
Charlemont, Massachusetts
413.337.4918
www.greenspacecollaborative.com

Engineers

Darcey Donovan, P.E.
Ecoengineering
Truckee, California
530.582.5516
ecoengr@sbcglobal.net

Eric Hasenoehrl, engineer
Lewiston, Idaho
208.743.2135

David Mar, Engineer
Tipping-Mar + Associates
Berkeley, California
510.549.1906
www.tippingmar.com

Ian Smith and Jeff Ruppert, P.E.
Odisea Engineering, Planning and
Consulting
Boulder, Colorado
303.443.4335
www.odiseanet.com

Internet Resources

BuildingGreen, LLC.
www.BuildingGreen.com
*Professionals source for unbiased information
on green design and construction materials.*

BuildingScience.com
buildingscience.com
*Objective, scientific information about
buildings, and what works.*

CREST SB Forum
http://listserv.repp.org/pipermail/
strawbale
*A lively online dialog of strawbale building,
with archive of previous discussions.*

European strawbale discussion list
(mostly in English)
http://amper.ped.muni.cz/mailman/listin
fo/strawbale

**Geiger Research Institute of
Sustainable Building**
www.grisb.org
*Online collection of straw-bale codes and
other resources.*

Healthy Building Network
www.healthybuilding.net
*Authoritative source for news about construc-
tion materials and health.*

Hybrid House Network
www.HybridHouse.com
*More photos, resources and updated informa-
tion, from the author of this book.*

The Last Straw Journal
www.thelaststraw.org
*Online source of U.S. and international
resources and information about natural
building.*

Natural Homes
www.naturalhomes.org/
*An interactive map of homes around the
world, with many links and resources.*

New Leaf America
www.NewLeafAmerica.com
*Online inspiration and step-by-step info
about efficiency products and services.*

Pattern Language Association
www.patternlanguage.com
*Tools for helping people to create beautiful,
functional, meaningful places.*

SB-R-US listserve
Online discussion group
groups.yahoo.com/groups/sb-r-us
SB-r-us-subscribe@yahoogroups.com

Sustainable Sources
www.greenbuilder.com
*Incl. Professionals Directory, Events
Calendar, and Straw-Bale Home Registry*

Wikipedia
http://en.wikibooks.org/wiki/Straw_Bale
_Construction
Online encyclopedia.

Home Plans

Straw Bale House Plans
www.strawbaleplans.wordpress.com

Open to the Public

Black Range Lodge B&B
Catherine Wanek, Owner
Kingston, New Mexico
575.895.5652
www.BlackRangeLodge.com
Strawbale guest house.

Earth Sweet Home Institute
Juliet Cuming and David Shaw
802.254.7674
www.earthsweethome.com

Heartwood Cohousing
Bayfield, Colorado
970.884.4055
www.heartwoodcohousing.com

Paca de Paja Bed & Breakfast
CarolineWilson, Innkeeper
Tucson, Arizona
520.822.2065 or 888.326.4588
www.pacadepaja.com

Pilgrim Holiness Church
Arthur, Nebraska
Arthur County Historical Society
County Clerk 308.764.2203

Organizations and Networks

Austrian StrawBale Network (ASBN)
www.baubiologie.at
Incl. Austria, Czech Republic, Slovakia,
Slovenia, Hungary, Germany

**California Straw Building
Association (CASBA)**
http://www.strawbuilding.org

The Cohousing Network
www.cohousing.org

**Colorado Straw Bale Association
(COSBA)**
http://www.coloradostrawbale.org

**The Ecological Building Network
(EBNet)**
www.ecobuildnetwork.org
*Extensive research on the properties of
strawbale structures. Many tests for free
download.*

French Straw-bale Forum
http://compaillons.naturalforum.net

**German Fachverband
Strohballenbau (FASBA)**
www.fasba.de

**MidAmerica Straw Bale Association
(MASBA)**
www.thelaststraw.org/sban.
*Center is in Nebraska (SBAN). Covering
IA, IL, IN, KS, MI, MN, MO, ND, SD,
& WI.*

Natural Builders Northeast (NBNE)
www.nbne.org
*Natural Building professionals throughout
the Northeastern U.S.*

The Northwest EcoBuilding Guild
www.ecobuilding.org
*Washington state regional association of sus-
tainable building.*

**Ontario Straw Bale Building
Coalition (OSBBC), Ontario, Canada**
www.osbbc.org

**The Southwest Natural Builders
Guild, Durango, CO**
www.swnaturalbuilders.com
*Experienced professionals in southwest
Colorado*

The Spanish Strawbale Network
www.casasdepaja.org

**The Straw Bale Association of Texas
(SBAT)**
www.greenbuilder.com/sbat

**Straw Bale Construction
Association of New Mexico (SBCA)**
www.strawbalecentral.com/SBCA

Publications

Environmental Building News
BuildingGreen, Inc.
802.257.7300
www.buildinggreen.com

The Last Straw Journal
The International Journal of
Strawbale and Natural Building
402.483.5135
www.thelaststraw.org
Articles, workshop calendar and resources.

Recommended Reading and Viewing

**More Straw Bale Building: A
Complete Guide to Planning and
Building with Straw**
Chris Magwood, Peter Mack, Tina
Therrien, New Society Publishers
(2005).
*Step-by-step guide to construction, with
essential information for planning: permit-
ting, budgeting, designing, drawing up
plans, and shopping for materials.*

**The Natural Plaster Book: Earth,
Lime and Gypsum Plasters for
Natural Homes**
Cedar Rose Guelberth & Dan Chiras,
New Society Publishers (2003).
*A how-to guide to design for, mix and apply
natural plasters in any climate.*

Small Strawbale
Athena Steen, Bill Steen, and Wayne
Bingham, Gibbs Smith, Publisher (2005).
*Colorful cottages, sheds, guest houses and tiny
dwellings present opportunities for experimentation and keeping the ecological
footprint modest.*

DVDs

Building with Awareness: The Construction of a Hybrid Home

Ted Owens, Syncronos Design.
www.buildingwithawareness.com
Artistic and detailed, showing the complete process of building a sustainable home with strawbale and adobe walls, solar panels, rainwater harvesting.

The Building with Straw Collection

Catherine Wanek, Black Range Films
www.strawbalecentral.com
Three early straw-bale videos on one DVD.

Vol. 1: A Straw-Bale Workshop—View post and beam straw-bale construction at a weekend workshop. Covers the basics of straw bale construction and the many different reasons that people are attracted to it (1993).

Vol. 2: A Straw-Bale Home Tour—Video tour of ten houses with a wide range of building styles, from a basic box to Santa Fe style, with owner interviews (1994).

Vol. 3: Straw-Bale Code Testing—Intended for building officials, this video will also be of interest to straw bale enthusiasts. Bale walls are subjected to compression and wind loads. Watch as a load-bearing strawbale wall is unloaded from a 2,000 degree furnace after two hours (1996).

Strawbale Workshops

The Canelo Project

Athena and Bill Steen
Elgin, Arizona
520.455.5548
www.caneloproject.com

Landerland Natural Building

Satomi and Tom Lander
Kingston, New Mexico
www.landerland.com

Solar Energy International

www.solarenergy.org
Offering hands-on workshops internationally